CURRENT STUDIES ON THE INDUS CIVILIZATION

RIHN-MANOHAR INDUS PROJECT SERIES

Current Studies on the Indus Civilization

VOLUME V

VIVEK DANGI

MANOHAR
2011

An earlier version of this work was published under the title
Linguistics, Archaeology and the Human Past (Occasional Paper 8)
in 2009, by Indus Project, Research Institute for
Humanity and Nature, Kyoto, Japan

This revised edition is now being
published as RIHN Library No. 18, 2011

ISBN 978-81-7304-859-3 (Series)
ISBN 978-81-7304-911-8 (Vol. V)

Published by
Ajay Kumar Jain for
Manohar Publishers & Distributors
4753/23 Ansari Road, Daryaganj
New Delhi 110 002

Printed at
Salasar Imaging Systems
Delhi 110 035

CONTENTS

Preface

Chapter I Nomenclature and Geographical Features 1

Chapter II Exploration 6

Chapter III Settlement Pattern 32

Chapter IV Study of Pottery 45

Chapter V Study of Miscellaneous Objects 70

Chapter VI Study of Coins and Inscriptions 88

Chapter VII Conclusion: History of the Region 105

References 110

LIST OF FIGURES

CHAPTER II

Figure 1 General map of Haryana
Figure 2 Explored sites in the Meham Block
Figure 3 Ajaib-1 General view
Figure 4 Bahelba-1 General view
Figure 5 Bedwa-1 General view
Figure 6 Bedwa-4 General view
Figure 7 Bedwa-5 General view
Figure 8 Bhaini Maharajpur General view
Figure 9 Bhaini Surjan-1 General view
Figure 10 Bhaini Surjan-1 General view
Figure 11 Bharan-1 General view
Figure 12 Farmana-1 General view
Figure 13 Farmana-3 General view
Figure 14 Ganganagar-1 General view
Figure 15 Girawad-1 General view
Figure 16 Kharkhra-1 General view
Figure 17 Madina-3 General view
Figure 18 Madina-5 General view
Figure 19 Meham Medieval structure
Figure 20 Meham-1 Habitational mound
Figure 21 Seman Medieval temple
Figure 22 Seman-5 General view

CHAPTER III

Figure 23 Distribution of pre-Harappan or Hakra Culture sites
Figure 24 Distribution of Early Harappan sites
Figure 25 Distribution of Mature Harappan sites
Figure 26 Distribution of Late Harappan sites
Figure 27 Distribution of PGW sites
Figure 28 Distribution of Early Historical and Historical sites

CHAPTER IV

Figure 29 Pre-Harappan Pottery from the Meham Block
Figure 30 Early Harappan Pottery from Bedwa-2
Figure 31 Early Harappan pottery from Farmana-1
Figure 32 Early Harappan pottery from the Meham Block
Figure 33 Mature Harappan pottery from Farmana-1
Figure 34 Mature Harappan pottery from the Meham Block
Figure 35 Mature Harappan Pottery from Kheri Meham
Figure 36 Late Harappan pottery from Farmana-1
Figure 37 Mature or Late Harappan Pottery from Bedwa-2
Figure 38 Late Harappan Pottery from Bedwa-2
Figure 39 Late Harappan Pottery from Bedwa-2
Figure 40 Late Harappan Pottery from Bedwa-2
Figure 41 Late Harappan Pottery from Kheri Meham
Figure 42 PGW from the Meham Block
Figure 43 PGW from Madina-2
Figure 44 PGW from Madina-2
Figure 45 PGW from the Meham Block
Figure 46 Black Slipped Ware from Madina-2
Figure 47 PGW from Madina-2
Figure 48 Early Historical and Historical pottery from the Meham Block
Figure 49 Historical pottery from Madina-IV
Figure 50 Historical pottery from the Meham Block
Figure 51 Early Medieval and Medieval pottery from the Meham Block
Figure 52 Medieval Pottery from Meham-2
Figure 53 Terracotta Cakes from the Meham Block

CHAPTER V

Figure 54 Terracotta wheels, toy cart frames and ear-stud from the Meham Block
Figure 55 Terracotta beads from the Meham Block
Figure 56 Terracotta discs and skin rubbers from the Meham Block
Figure 57 Terracotta animal figurine from Bahelba-2

Figure 58 Terracotta animal figurine from Bahelba-2
Figure 59 Terracotta animal figurines from Farmana-1 (3-4) and Meham-2 (5)
Figure 60 Teracotta animal figurine from Meham-2
Figure 61 Stone balls from the Meham Block
Figure 62 Stone pestles from the Meham Block
Figure 63 Chert tools and object from the Meham Block
Figure 64 Copper objects from the Meham Block
Figure 65 Copper spearhead from the Meham Block
Figure 66 Gold and bone objects from the Meham Block
Figure 67 Beads from the Meham Block
Figure 68 Beads and disc from the Meham Block
Figure 69 Faience and terracotta bangles from the Meham Block

CHAPTER VI

Figure 70 Kushana coins from Madina-4
Figure 71 Kushana coins from Madina-4
Figure 72 Kushana coins from Madina-4
Figure 73 Kushana coins from Madina-4
Figure 74 Kushana coins from Madina-4
Figure 75 Kushana coins from Madina-4
Figure 76 Kushana coins from Madina-4
Figure 77 Kushana coins from Madina-4
Figure 78 Kushana coins from Madina-4
Figure 79 Kushana coins from Madina-4
Figure 80 Kushana coins from Madina-4
Figure 81 Kushana coins from Madina-4
Figure 82 Yaudheya and Medieval coins
Figure 83 Yaudheya and Medieval coins

CHAPTER VII

Figure 84 Graph showing site-wise distribution of sites in the Meham Block

LIST OF TABLES

Table 1 Number of sites during different cultural periods
Table 2 Number of sites in respect of size during different cultural periods
Table 3 Total number of sites and area occupied by each category of sites
Table 4 Mean settlement size during different cultural periods
Table 5 Number of settlements of different categories in the Meham Block
Table 6 Average population per km^2 during different cultural periods
Table 7 Mean population per settlement during different cultural periods
Table 8 Estimate of population in the Meham Block during different cultural periods

Figure 58 Terracotta animal figurine from Bahelba-2
Figure 59 Terracotta animal figurines from Farmana-1 (3-4) and Meham-2 (5)
Figure 60 Teracotta animal figurine from Meham-2
Figure 61 Stone balls from the Meham Block
Figure 62 Stone pestles from the Meham Block
Figure 63 Chert tools and object from the Meham Block
Figure 64 Copper objects from the Meham Block
Figure 65 Copper spearhead from the Meham Block
Figure 66 Gold and bone objects from the Meham Block
Figure 67 Beads from the Meham Block
Figure 68 Beads and disc from the Meham Block
Figure 69 Faience and terracotta bangles from the Meham Block

CHAPTER VI

Figure 70 Kushana coins from Madina-4
Figure 71 Kushana coins from Madina-4
Figure 72 Kushana coins from Madina-4
Figure 73 Kushana coins from Madina-4
Figure 74 Kushana coins from Madina-4
Figure 75 Kushana coins from Madina-4
Figure 76 Kushana coins from Madina-4
Figure 77 Kushana coins from Madina-4
Figure 78 Kushana coins from Madina-4
Figure 79 Kushana coins from Madina-4
Figure 80 Kushana coins from Madina-4
Figure 81 Kushana coins from Madina-4
Figure 82 Yaudheya and Medieval coins
Figure 83 Yaudheya and Medieval coins

CHAPTER VII

Figure 84 Graph showing site-wise distribution of sites in the Meham Block

LIST OF TABLES

Table 1 Number of sites during different cultural periods
Table 2 Number of sites in respect of size during different cultural periods
Table 3 Total number of sites and area occupied by each category of sites
Table 4 Mean settlement size during different cultural periods
Table 5 Number of settlements of different categories in the Meham Block
Table 6 Average population per km^2 during different cultural periods
Table 7 Mean population per settlement during different cultural periods
Table 8 Estimate of population in the Meham Block during different cultural periods

Chapter VI deals with coins and inscriptions, and the following Chapter VII deals with history of the region.

Acknowledgements

This research work is a result of my deep appreciation and love of the ancient cultures of Haryana, especially Rohtak district.

First of all, I express my deep sense of gratitude and heart-felt thanks to my research supervisor Dr. Sukhdev Saini, Department of Ancient Indian History Culture and Archaeology, Kurukshetra University, Kurukshetra for his benign kindness and providing proper guidance to me.

It is my pleasant duty to acknowledge many individuals who enlightened me during my field work Dr. Manmohan Kumar, Professor and Head, Department of History, M.D. University, Rohtak, Haryana, India, Shri G.B. Sharma, retired archaeological officer, Government of Punjab, and Prof. Vasant Shinde, Department of Archaeology, Deccan College Post-Gradate and Research Institute, India, Prof. Nirmal Kayshap, Department of History, M.D. University, Rohtak, Haryana, India, Dr. Akinori Uesugi of Research Institute for Humanity and Nature Kyoto, Japan, and Dr. J.S. Kharakwal, Institute of Rajasthan Studies, J.R.N. Rajasthan Vidyapeeth, Udaipur, India, Mr. Vikas Pawar and Ms. Neha Kothari for their support, valuable suggestion and encouragement. They encouraged me to undertake careful documentation of the sites. They were kind to read my manuscript with great care and provide their valuable comments. The text was improved considerably after their comments. However, I am alone responsible for all short comings. I owe some photographs in this monograph to Mr. Pradeep Kumar.

I would like to express my gratitude to my friend Mr. Appu and his family. He not only accompanied me during my entire field work but also provided cultural material in his collection for study. During my field work Appu's mother took special care of our food and all other needs whereas his father Mr. Jai Singh Sharan, former Village Chief (Sarpanch) of Bedwa, was a great source of encouragement for field work.

Words would fail to express my heart-felt sentiment for the love, blessing and encouragement that I have received from my parents, brother, sister (Ms. Suman) and brother-in-law (Mr. Sanjay). They have been a tremendous source of inspiration and motivation for me.

Last but not least, I am also thankful to Prof. Toshiki Osada, the Leader of the Indus Project, Research Institute for Humanity and Nature Kyoto, Japan, for accepting my work for publication and for giving the author valuable suggestions and support.

Vivek Dangi
M.D. University, Rohtak,
Haryana, India
vivek_dangi@yahoo.co.in

Preface by the Author

'Archaeology of the Ghaggar Basin: Settlement Archaeology of Meham Block (Rohtak), Haryana' is a revised version of my dissertation submitted to Department of Ancient Indian History, Culture and Archaeology, Kurukshetra University, Kurukshetra, Haryana, India, for the award of Master of Philosophy Degree. The region under present study is confined to the Meham Block of the Rohtak District, Haryana, India. I chose this topic because of the important site of Farmana, which I explored thoroughly and noticed that it was a full-fledged urban center during the Harappan times. Its size, material culture and location is very important because it is located about 25 km southeast of Rakhigarhi and about 13 km north of Mitathal. The basic aim of the present research work was to study its catchment area and its ecological relationship. But when I explored the region, I got a good number of sites around Farmana and my main focus was to highlight the archaeological importance of the region. Besides this, I found some Harappan cemetery belong to the Late Harappan period which are quite unique in the protohistoric archaeology of Haryana. The present dissertation aims at collection and study of all available archeological data for the reconstruction of the settlement pattern of this region. While the main focus was on the settlement pattern and systematic analysis, it was necessary to provide a comprehensive but brief and updated account of the protohistoric, historic and medieval cultures of the Meham Block. These cultures have been discussed in such a way that not only the archeological history of the area emerges but also the personality of each culture comes out clearly. The main source of material is provided by explorations either by the previous explorers or by the author. In addition, both excavated and explored materials from the adjoining areas and ethnographic data is also used as source material for the present work.

However, I am aware of the limitations and the methodological problems involved with this kind of work. This work deals with a small area having almost the same ecological condition. In fact not even a single site was excavated in the study area when I began the field work. Recently excavations at three sites, viz. Farmana, Girawad and Madina have begun. This dissertation deals with the settlement pattern of 68 archeological sites in the jurisdiction of the Meham Block.

Chapter I deals with nomenclature and geographical and echological background of the region. Besides, this chapter also deals with the location of the study area, topography, soils, climate, temperature, flora, fauna, people, languages, etc. of the region. Chapter II presents the details of archaeological field work conducted by the present researcher in the region. In addition to the data of the field research, the location of study area and sites, geo-coordinates, size of the sites, cultural sequence and local name are also given. Chapter III deals with the settlement pattern, approximate population at each site, frequency of sites and intra-site relationship. Chapter IV illustrates the analysis of pottery belonging to different cultures, with special reference to shapes, fabric and decorations. Chapter V presents a brief description of miscellaneous finds from various settlements.

PREFACE

I am very happy to announce the publication of the fifth volume of the RIHN-Manohar Indus project series.

India has a long tradition of archaeology. The Archaeological Survey of India has led the research in this field since Harappa and Mohenjo Daro were excavated by Daya Ram Sahni and Rakal Das Banerji, respectively, under the direction of John Marshall. It seems to me, however, that recent archaeological research, especially concerning Harappan sites, has, to my regret, not been able to progress much. It was perhaps due to the lack of proper training which should have been given to the scholars of new generations. Besides, due to the influence of 'globalization' spreading even in the academic world, scholars tend to turn their backs on painstaking field research in remote areas nowadays.

In this academic climate I met Vivek Dangi. He is a young postgraduate student from M.D. University, Rohtak, Haryana, and is one of the most active field workers in India. He loves antiquities and old things of any kind. He and his friends have travelled extensively exploring many archaeological sites including Harappan ones in Haryana. As a result they have discovered hundreds of new Harappan sites there. They reminded me of the so-called 'kooko-shoonen' (boys crazy for archaeological discoveries) found particularly in the post-war Japan. Some of them became famous archaeologists later and laid the foundation of archaeological research in Japan.

Vivek is still in his twenties. Whatever difficulties he will face in his research, I, believe that his energy and enthusiasm will carry him through. This thesis is just a starting point. I hope he and his friends will continue their work and explore the Harappan culture not only in Haryana but also in other parts of South Asia, and make a significant contribution to the revival of the Indian archaeological tradition in the future.

Toshiki Osada

Project Leader and Professor
Research Institute for Humanity and Nature
Kyoto, Japan

CHAPTER 1

NOMENCLATURE AND GEOGRAPHICAL FEATURES

Meham is a block and a tehsil headquarter of the Rohtak District in Haryana. It derives its name from the headquarter town of Meham and is one of the five blocks of the Rohtak District. Meham is situated about 30 km west of Rohtak on the Delhi-Fazilka National Highway no.10. The nomenclature of Meham has been variously explained in local traditions. According to one tradition which is still prevalent among people, the town was completely destroyed by Durga Dass during the reign of Aurangzeb. Thereafter, a man named Mandu 'Dhobi' settled here and after him this place was called Mandu and later corrupted as 'Meham'. The inscription of the Pirzada Mosque, which can be dated to 1641 ACE (AH 1051) refers to the name of this place as Mahim. The present name Meham is its still modified version.

In *Mahabharata* a place name Mahittna is referred to (*Mahabharata* II: 3-5), which is situated to the west of Rohitiki (Rohtak), the capital of the Yaudheya republic. This place can be identified with the modern Meham town. In *Mahabharata* it is mentioned that Nakul, the Pandava warrior, conquered ten forts to the west of Khandava-Parastha. Mittittna (Meham) was one of them (*Mahabharata* II: 29).

The Meham Block lies between 28°52' to 29°05' north latitude and 76°13' to 76°29' east longitude. It spreads over an area of about 419 km^2, which comprises the township of Meham and 24 villages. The block is bounded by the Lakhan-Majra Block of the Rohtak District on the east, the Hansi Block-II of the Hisar District on the west, the Julana Block of the Jind District on the north, the Kalanuar Block of the Rohtak District on the south and southeast, the Mundhal Block of the Bhiwani District on the south and the Bhiwani Block on the southwest.

TOPOGRAPHY

The region under the present study is a part of alluvial plain and a part of the Indo-Gangetic Plain. The topography of the region owes its existence to geomorphic process having closer affinity to the arid climate, both in the recent and past geological periods. This Indo-Gangetic Plain is formed by the deposition of the alluvial sediments brought by the rivers from the Himalayas into the trough between the great Himalayas in the north and the Deccan Plateau in the south. This deposit is known as '*Bhangara*', which is the older alluvium to the age of the Pleistocene period. It generally occupies the higher ground, which is too elevated to be flooded by the present rivers such as the Ghaggar and Yamuna (Duggal 1970: 3). Physiographically, it is an 'upland plain or the Ghaggar-Yamuna doab' which is almost a level plain, ranging in height from 220 to 280 m above the sea level. In general, it slopes gently from northeast to southwest (Duggal 1970: 8). But during the flood of 1995 the water moved from northeast to southeast. The villages on the western side of the Meham Block like Bedwa, Seman, Bhaini Surjan, Bhaini Chanderpal, Bhaini Matoo, Bhaini Maharajpur, Bhaini Bharo have very high sand-dunes, some of which have an height of more than 30 m. These sand-dunes reveal that in past on these places there must have been a river. The rests of the villages are siatuted on the alluvial plain.

MINERAL RESOURCES

The area under study is not rich in mineral resources. The minerals found in the area are as given below.

Kankar

Kankar occurs at several places in the sandy tracts of

block. It is used for road metalling and as building material.

Saltpetre

Saltpetre occurs as very thin whitish yellow, brittle encrustations over the soil, and along the basement of *kaccha* constructions in some old and deserted villages. The efflorescence normally appears during the hot months from April to June every year. After the rains, it completely disappears, being washed away in solutions, partly as run off and partly by percolation down into the sandy soils, where the nitrates perhaps get denitrified. It is noteworthy that the nitrates are mostly concentrated in the top soil only. Many refineries exist in the area for extractions of saltpetre (most of them are located on archaeological sites).

UNDERGROUND WATER

The sub-soil water of the area under present study is sweet and brackish. The quality of water varies from place to place. The introduction of extensive canal irrigation caused rapid increase in water table. The water table in the Meham Block is 5 m below surface. But during the rainy season it comes above surface.

SOIL

The flat and featureless plain of the area is covered by a deep deposition of alluvial soil. The main components of the soil are sand and clay. The *rausli* soil and sand are the type of soil, which are found in this area. These are fairly good for the cultivation, provided that adequate rainfall or irrigation is received.

CROPS

The majority of the people of the area, mainly depend upon agriculture. But farming still continues to be a big gamble depending upon weather conditions. There are mainly two harvests in a year, viz. the *rabi* locally called *sadhru* (*sadhu*) that is winter sowing. The major *rabi* crops are wheat, gram, barley, mustard, tafamra, berseem, methi, tobacco, potatoes and other vegetables. In sandy area only *sadhru* is sown. The *kharif* is locally called '*sammu*'. The kharif crop consists chiefly of sugarcane, cotton, jowar, bajra, gawara, paddy, maiz, moong, moth, mash, san and ground net. (Haryana District Gazetteer, Rohtak 1970: 71)

IRRIGATION

The sources of irrigation in this region are tube-wells, canals and rainfall. The canal irrigation in this region is provided by the Bhiwani feeder canal and Jui canal. Besides both of these canals, there are some minor canals, which provide water for irrigation. The canals and minors do not cover the whole area and even in the area so covered the intensity of irrigation is not sufficient to produce two crops annually. Presently, the underground water level in this area is not so deep, so tube-wells are a good source of irrigation. Irrigation in the sand dunes totally depends upon tube-wells and rainfall.

TEMPERATURE

There are seasonal variations in the temperature records. The temperature begins to increase in March and continues to increase towards the end of June when it reaches upto 47 °C or 48 °C. With the advent of monsoon approximately in the end of June, there is an appreciable fall in the day temperature and the weather becomes cooler during the summer season. After the withdrawal of the monsoon in the later half of September, the temperature begins to decrease. The decrease in the temperature becomes rapid after October. January is generally the coldest month with the mean daily maximum temperature at 21.7 °C and the mean daily minimum temperature at 5.50 °C (Haryana District Gazetteer, Rohtak 1970: 17-18). In the year of 2005, it was very cold that the upper level of ponds was frozen. In the cold season the region is affected by cold winds in the wake of the passing western disturbances and minimum temperature drops down to sub-zero temperature.

HUMIDITY

The moisture content in the air is maximum in July and August, but the period of its high percentage is generally from July to September. The humidity declines in two phases, first from September to October and second from December to March, while in August the rise in humidity is quite rapid.

RAINFALL AND CLOUDINESS

Meham has an annual rainfall of 80 cm. The annual rainfall during the years of 1982, 1983 and 1984 was recorded as 75.36 cm, 88.24 cm and 63.14 cm respectively. About 74 % of annual rainfall occurs during the southwest monsoon in the month of June-July (Statistical Summary of District Rohtak, 1984-85: 21). There is a significant amount of rainfall in the month of June in the form of thundershowers and in the rest of the year there is very little rainfall. In the month of January there is also good rainfall due to the western disturbances from Pakistan. During the monsoon season, the sky is mostly moderate to heavily cloudy. The rest of the year, the sky is generally clear or lightly cloudy. Cloudy sky prevails for brief spells of the day or two in association with the passing western disturbances in the cold seasons.

WINDS

Winds are generally slow during the post-monsoon period and winter months. They are strengthened a little during the summer and monsoon months. They are predominantly easterly or southeasterly in the monsoon season and mostly westerly or northwesterly in other season. During summer season, dry winds locally called '*loo*' blow at high speeds and is totally dry and hot.

PEOPLE AND LANGUAGE

About 90% of the total population is rural. The Hindus, Muslims, Sikhs and Christians constitute the major portion of the population, of which Jats are the dominant while Banias, Jogis, Kumharas (potters), Nai (barbers), Sainis (malis), Sunrars (goldsmith) and Chamars are in the minority in villages. In the Meham town, refugee migrants from western Punjab (Pakistan) at the time of partition of India in 1947 are dominant.

Haryanavi or the Jatu is the major dialect spoken all over the region. Migrants from Pakistan speak Jhangi (Punjabi). Hindi in Devanagari script is used for writing purpose by an ever-increasing number of peoples.

FAUNA

Due to the growing population, the expansion of cultivation, and the reclamation of jungles and barren lands, wild animals are disappearing very fast. Thus finding no refuge and shelter, animals and birds have migrated and are still migrating to other places. However, a few wild animals are still found in the region. Animals found in the region are given below.

Mammals

Rhesus macaque or Bandar (*Macaca mulatta*), Common langur (*Presbytis entellus*), Common Mongoose (*Herpestes edwardsi*), Jackal (*Canis aureus*), Indian fox (*Vulpes bengtalenis*), Stripped hyaena (*Hyaena hyaena*), Bheriya (*Canis lupus*), Grey musk-shrew or chuchunder (*Suncus murinus*), Common yellow bat (*Scotophilus heathi*), Tickell's bat (*Hesperoptenus tickelli*), Five stripped palm squirrel or gilheri (*Funambulus pennanti*), Indian porcupine or sahi (*Hystrix indica*), Common house rats (*Rattus rattus*), House mouse (*Mus musculus*), Indian hare (*Lepus nigricollis*), Chinkara or ravine deer (*Gazella gazelle*), Blackbuck (*Antilope cervicapara*), Bluebull or nilgai (*Boselaphus tragocamelus*).

Birds

Brahminy duck (*Tadorna ferruginea*), Common shelduck (*Tadorna tadorna*), Pintail (*Anas acuta*), Mallard (*Anas platyrhynchos*), Wigeon (*Anas Fenelope*), Bluewinged teal (*Anas querquedula*),

Ferruginous duck (*Aythya fuligula*), Tufted duck (*Aytha fuligula*), Comb duck (*Sakidiornis melanotos* melanotos), Cotton teal (*Nettapus coromandelianus coromandelianus*), Spotbill duck (*Anas poecilorhyncha*), Tree duck (*Dendrocygna javanica*), Black partridge (*Francolinus francolinus asiae*), Grey partridge (*Francolinus pondicerianus interpositus*), Grey quail (*Coturnix coturnix coturnix*), Blue rock pigeon (*Columba livia*), Western turtle dove (*Streptopelia orientalis meena*), Indian ring dove (*Streptopelia decaocto decaocto*), Indian spotted dove (*Streptopelia chinesis suratensis*), Pariah kite (*Milvus migrams*), King vulture (*Torgos calvus*), Tawny eagle (*Aquila rapax vindiana*), House crow (*Corvus splendens*), Indian jungle crow (*Corvus macrorhynchos cluminatus*), Indian shikra (*Accipiter badius dussumieri*), Lagger flacon (*Falco biarmicus*), Redheaded merlin (*Falco chicquera chicquera*), Eagle owl (*Bubo bubo*), Mottle wood owl (*Strix ocellata*), Indian house swift (*Apus affinis affinis*), Indian grey shrike (*Lanius excubitor lahtora*), Indian baybacked shrike (*Lanius vittatus vittatus*), King crow (*Dicrurus adsimilis albirictus*), Indian pied myna (*Sturnus contra contra*), Indian myna (*Acridotheres gininianus*), Bank myna (*Acridotheres gininianus*), Northern jungle myna (*Acridotheres fuscus fuscus*), Northern goldenbacked woodpeckers (*Dinopium benghalense benghalense*), Koel (*Eudynamys scolopacea scolopacea*), Indian pied kingfisher (*Ceryle rudis leucomelantra*), Redvented bulbul (*Pycnonotus cafer*), Indian purple sunbird (*Estrilda amendava amandava*) and Indian small green bee-easter (Merops philippinus philippinus).

Reptiles

Common Indian krait (*Elapide Bungarus caeruleus*), Phoorsa (*Echis carinatus*), Indain python (*molurus*), John's sand boa (*Eryx johni johni*), Rat snake (*Ptyas mucosus*), Sand snake (*Psammgphis leithi*), Common lizards (*Haemidactylus brooki*), Kirla or girgit (*Calotes versicolour*), Sanda (*Uromastix hardwicki*).

Amphibians

Tortoises (*Geoclemys hamitloni* (ii) *Kachuga dhongoka*), Indian bull frog (*Ranidae Rana tigrina*), Indian cricket frog (*Rana Limnocharis*), Indian burrowing frog (*Rana breviceps*), Common toad (*Bufonidae Bufo melanostictus*), Parri (*Notopterus notopterus*), Katla (*Catla catla*), Mrigal (*Cirrhinus reba*), Bata (*Labeo bata*), Siriha (*Labeo gonius*), Rohu (*Labeo rohita*), Magur (*Clarias batrachus*), Singhara (*Mystus seenghala*), Ghally (*Ompok bimaculatus*), Mallee (*Wallago attu*) and Dolla (*Channa punetatus*),

FLORA

The forests of the block fall under the category of tropical desert thorn and comprise predominantly xerophytes. Flora is scanty and sparse. The floral types found in the area under study are as below.

Jand (*Prosopis cineraria*), Rohera (*Tecomella undulate*), Khairi (*Acacia Senegal*), Beri (*Zizphus mauritiana*), Reru (*Acacia Leucophloea*), Jal or van (*Salvadora oleoides* Decne), Barh (*Ficus bengalensis* L.), Peepal (*Ficus religiosa* L.), Mesquite or pahari kikar (*Prosopis juliflora*), Kachnar (*Bauhinia racemosa Lamk*), Amaltas (*Cassia fistula* L.), Lasura (*Cordia dichotema*), Imli (*Tamarindus indica* L.), Banna (*Cratava adansoni*), Shisham (*Dalbergia sissoo* Roxb.) Kikar (*Acacia nilotica*), Neem (*Azadirachta indica* Juss. Syn. *Melia azadirachta* L.), Gulmohar (Delonix regia).

Shrubs

Hins (*Capparis septaria* L. *Carissa spinarum* L.), Castor (*Ricinus Communis*), Panwar (*Cassia tora* L. (ii) *Cassia occidentalis* L.), Babool (*Acacia jacquemontii Benth*), Mallah (*Zizyphus nummularia*), Karir (*Capparis deciduas*), Khip (*Leptadenia pyrotechnica*), Ak (*Calotropis procera*).

Medicinal Plants

Bansa (*Adhatoda vasida Nees*), Indirain (*Citrullus colocynthis*), Asgandha (*Withania somnifera*), Glo

(*Tinospera cordifolia Miers*), Kharuthi (*Sida acuta Burm.*), Dhatura *(Datura stramonium*), Bhakhra (*Tribulus terrestrial*).

Grasses

Anjan (*Cenchrus ciliaris*), Dhaman (*Cenchrus setigerus Vahl*), Dub (*Cynodon dactylon*), Kana (*Saccharum bengalense*), Dabh (*Desmostachya bipinnatta*).

CHAPTER II

EXPLORATION

The region under the present study is very rich in archaeological wealth. In order to obtain the material culture remains of the past cultures/civilizations, the present researcher conducted an extensive village-to-village survey of the Meham Block, Rohtak District (Haryana) during May, June and July in 2006 (Figure 1).

Silak Ram was responsible for initiating archaeological investigations in the area and brought to light some sites from this area during his research (Silak Ram 1972). Shila Devi though did not explore the area but brought to light some sculptures from Meham for the same purposes (Shila Devi 1975: Pl.XXX-E). Later in 1989, Surender Singh conducted an archaeological exploration for his M.Phil. research work and discovered a good number of new sites (Surender Singh 1989: 13-27). Recently Dr. Manmohan Kumar from Department of History, M.D. University, Rohtak brought to light some sites (Manmohan Kumar 2005-06: 196-204).

With this archaeological background of the region, the present researcher explored this region. As a result of this effort 68 sites were explored out of which 38 sites were placed on the archaeological map for the first time (Figure 2). These sites range from the Hakra Culture to the Medieval times. As most of the sites are under cultivation, not even a single site is intact in a full sense. Pottery and other associated finds of different cultures were collected from the sites for the study of different aspects of the cultures.

The distribution of cultural assemblage of Meham block is as given below.

Cultural assemblage	*No. of sites*
Pre-Harappan (or Hakra)	3
Early Harappan	8
Mature Harappan	7
Late Harappan	30
Painted Grey Ware (PGW)	22
Early Historical and Historical	23
Medieval	37

All the archaeological sites in this region are arranged alphabetically and described briefly with location, size and cultural bearing in the following pages.

AJAIB

The Ajaib village is located about 20 km northeast of the Meham town and about same distance west of the Rohtak city. A link road from Madina on the Rohtak-Hisar Road leads to the village. There are two archaeological sites in the jurisdiction of this village. Both sites were initially discovered by Surender Singh (1989: 14-15).

1 AJAIB-1 (76°30'25"N, 29°07'15"E)

The site Ajaib-1 (Figure 3) lies at distance of 500 m north of the village on the Ajaib-Bansi Road. This site is locally known as Khera. The owner of the land is Shri Rattan Singh, s/o Shri Molar Ram. This site falls in the saline wasteland. It measures about 2 ha and it is almost as low as the surrounding field level due to the removal of soil. All over the mounds, sherds of Late Harappan and PGW are found. Main shapes included vases, storage jars, bowls, dishes, etc. The antiquities recovered from the site include *ghata*-shaped bead and two faience beads.

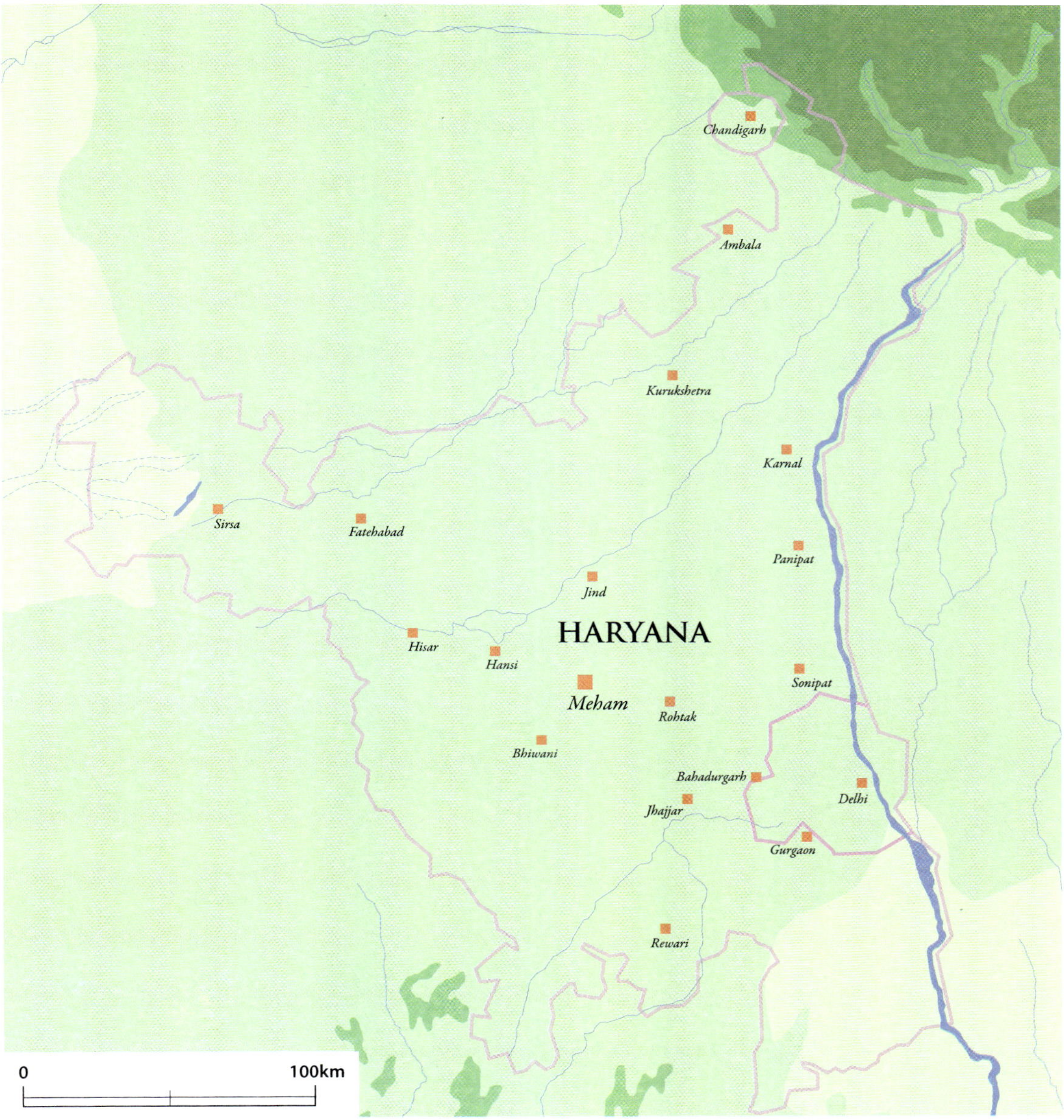

Figure 1 General map of Haryana

2 AJAIB-2 (76°30'50"N, 29°06'45"E)

This site is located about 100 m southeast of the village and east of water-work complex. It is locally known as Khera. The site is spread over an area about 1.2 ha and it is about 0.5 m high from the surrounding ground level. The owner of the land is Shri Balwant Singh, s/o Shri Sher Singh. During the explorations the site yielded red ware and red slipped ware with the main shapes of bowls, vases and carinated *handis*. On the basis of these finds, this site may be assigned to the Medieval periods.

BAHELBA

This village is located about 5 km southeast of the Meham town and about 25 km west of Rohtak. An approachable road from the Rohtak-Hisar Road (NH no.10) near the Kharkhra village leads to the village. There are three archaeological sites in the revenue area of the village.

Figure 2 Explored sites in the Meham Block

3 BAHELBA-1 (76°23'29"N, 29°01'45")

This archaeological site (Figure 4) is situated at a distance of about 1 km south of the village. The owner of the land is Shri Chajju Ram and locally this is known as Khera. It measures about 3.5 ha and about 2 m high from the surrounding field level. During the exploration the site yielded PGW, Black-Slipped Ware (BSW), Grey Ware (GW), red ware and red slip ware. On the basis of these finds, it can be suggested that the site was occupied during the PGW period and Kushana period. Besides pottery, a copper object was also found during the exploration.

4 BAHELBA-2 (76°23'20"N, 29°01'00"E)

This site is located about 2 km south of the village and about 100 m west of the Bhiwani feader canal. This site is close to Kheri-ali-Mori and is locally known as Kheri. It measures about 1.5 ha. There is no trace of the mound at present. The whole mound has been levelled by the farmers to make the land available for cultivation. The owner of the land is Shri Mehar Singh, s/o Shri Baharat Singh. This site yielded evidence of the Early Harrapan and Historical periods. This is a new site which is being placed on the archaeological map for the first time.

Figure 3 Ajaib-1 General view

Figure 4 Bahelba-1 General view

5 BAHELBA-3 (76°22'15"N, 28°50'00"E)

This site lies about 5 km southeast of the village. This site falls in the revenue jurisdiction of two villages, i.e. Bahelba and Kilanga (Bhiwani District). This site is quite large and intact. The site spreads over an area of about 6.5 ha and about 3 m high from the surrounding ground level. This site yielded evidence of the Late Harappan, PGW, Historical and Medieval periods. Fragments of faience bangles and beads were collected from the site during exploration. This site was initially discovered by Surender Singh (1989: 15-16).

BEDWA

The Bedwa village is located about 13 km north of the Meham town. An approachable road on the Meham-Julana Road bifurcating from Farmana leads to the village. There are five archaeological sites with in the revenue jurisdiction of the village.

6 BEDWA-1 (76°20'10"N, 29°14'07"E)

The archaeological site Bedwa-1 (Figure 5), is located close to the village and behind Government Middle School and the Bedwa-Puthi Road passes through the site. It is locally known as Kurada. This site occupies an area of about 4 ha and it is now 7 m high from the surrounding field level. On the whole mound, sherds of Historical and Medieval periods are found. In past, Surender Singh reported only Medieval remains here (Surender Singh 1989: 16). But present researcher discovered Historical remains for the first time.

7 BEDWA-2 (76°20'02"N, 29°14'00"E)

There is another site about 350 m southwest of the village on sand-dunes. While removing the sand from the dunes, villagers found some potsherds along the human bones. The villagers contacted Mr. Appu, a M.A. student of the Department of History, M.D. University, Rohtak. He soon informed his teachers and the student along with his teacher visited the site.

Figure 5 Bedwa-1 General view

Figure 6 Bedwa-4 General view

Figure 7 Bedwa-5 General view

At this stage, it was found that the remains belonged to a cemetery of the Harappan times (*Dainik Bhaskar*, Dec. 13, 2005). According to Dr. Manmohan Kumar, Reader from the Department of History, M.D. University Rohtak, this cemetery belongs to early Late Harappan period or late phase of the Mature Harappan period.

During the course of removing sand from the site, at least 50 graves with grave goods were noticed. The bodies were laid in the north-south direction with their heads towards north and near the head grave goods (pottery) were placed. Normally four pots of different sizes consisting of bowls, dish-on-stands with a long stem and *lota*-shaped pots were placed. With above-mentioned pottery types, some other types like vases of elliptical shape, perforated jar, spherical collarless pot, miniature pots and small beakers were also found. Although the bulk of pottery is unpainted, some painted pottery were also recovered. Paintings were mainly black bands of various sizes around neck and body of the pot. Some pots with wavy lines were also found.

One collarless pot which is painted by various motifs includes peacock and other floral designs is included in the collection. This pot contained ash and bones. This type of urn burial has also been reported from Cemetery H at Harappa. Thus we can conclude that both complete burials and fractional burials were in practice. The evidence from this site indicated that cremation of the dead bodies was also conducted, the ash and few selected bones being buried in an urn.

The pottery found from the site belong to the Late Harappan tradition. But some pots give an idea of the Mature Harappan elements, e.g. long-stemmed dish-on-Stand, perforated jars and beakers. But in conclusion we can say that this site belonged to the late phase of Mature Harappan phase and early phase of Late Harrappan period (Manmohan Kumar 2005: 198).

8 BEDWA-3 (76°19'30"N, 29°14'30"E)

This mound is located about 2 km west of the village and on the left side of the Bedwa-Puthi Road. It spreads over an area of about 2.30 ha and about 3 m high from the surroundings ground level. The whole site is under cultivation. The owner of the land is Shri Parthi Singh, s/o Shri Bhim Singh. It is locally known as Parthi-ali-Giradhi. The ceramic industries represented on the mound are PGW, BSW and stamped pottery of Early Historic period. During the exploration, fragments of faience bangles, a *ghata*-shaped bead, and a bead of lapis lazuli were also found.

9 BEDWA-4 (76°20'10"N, 29°14'30"E)

This site (Figure 6) lies about 500 m west of the village and on the right side of the Bedwa-Puthi Road. It is located on sand-dunes of about 6 m high. Potsherds were found in an area of about 5 ha. The ceramic industries represented are the red ware of the Medieval period. Common shapes include jars, storage jars, bowls, basins, etc. A bead of agate was also found in the course of exploration.

10 BEDWA-5 (76°26'40"N, 29°15'10"E)

There is another site of archaeological importance in the revenue area of the village (Figure 7). This site lies about 2.5 km northwest of the village on sand-dunes of about 4 m high and presently used for an agricultural purpose. It occupies an area of about 2 ha. Potsherds of the late Mature Harrapan period, similar to those from Bedwa-2, and Medieval pottery are found.

BHAINI CHANDERPAL

The village Bhaini Chanderpal is about 3 km north of the Meham town. This village is situated on the Meham-Julana Road. There is only one site in the revenue area of the village.

11 BHAINI CHANDERPAL

(76°20'00"N, 29°08'30"E)

This site is about 2 km west of the village. It is locally known as Burj. On the site there is a mud-brick tower, after which the site is named Burj. It measures about 2.5 ha in size and about 1 m high. Except the northern part of the site, the whole site is presently used for an agriculture purpose. The site has yielded red ware and red slipped ware, consisting of basins, spouted pots, knife-edge bowls, etc. On the basis of the shapes of above-mentioned ceramic industries the site may be placed under the Historical and Medieval periods.

BHAINI MAHARAJPUR

The village Bhaini Maharajpur is about 5 km west of the Meham town on NH no.10. This village is locally known as Mill-ali-Bhaini as the Meham Sugar Mill is situated in the revenue area of the village.

12 BHAINI MAHARAJPUR-1

(76°14'45"N, 29°06'45"E)

This site (Figure 8) is located about 1 km west of the village and about 700 m south of the sugar mill. It is situated on a sandy area and the whole site is under cultivation. The northern portion of the site was removed about 1.8 m deep for an agriculture purpose. The potsherds spread over an area of about 2 ha. This site has yielded pottery similar to those from Bedwa-2, i.e. late Mature Harappan or early Late Harappan periods. Besides it has also yielded Historical pottery.

BHAINI SURJAN

The village Bhaini-Surjan is situated about 5 km north of the Meham town. An approachable road from Meham leads to the village. There are three ancient sites within the revenue are of the village.

Figure 8 Bhaini Maharajpur General view

13 BHAINI SURJAN-1 (76°17'30"N, 29°08'15"E)
This site (Figures 9 and 10) is located about 1 km west of the village on sand-dunes, which are of about 17 m in height. The Bhaini Surjan-Bhaini Matoo Road passes through this site. It falls in the barren land and lies in the *panchayati* land. This site was discovered by Surender Singh, but he only identified medieval remains here (Surender Singh 1989:16). It measures 5 ha in size. The ceramic evidence found here is red ware which belongs to the Late Harappan and Medieval periods. The Late Harappan remains from this site are found for the first time by the present researcher.

14 BHAINI SURJAN-2 (76°16'05"N, 29°08'10"E)
The archaeological site Bhaini Surjan-2 lies about 1.5 km north of the village and about 500 m southwest of a government highschool. A cart-track from the Bhaini Surjan-Seman Road leads to the site. This site is located on sand-dunes and locally known as Tibbi (low sand-dunes). Potsherds are found over an area of about 2 ha. The owner of the land is Shri Kapoor, s/o Shri Shibba. The ceramic evidence found here is the same as those found from Bedwa-2, i.e. late Mature Harappan or early Late Harappan. During the course of levelling the site, a number of bones and human skulls were also found, indicating that there was a cemetery on this site. This type of cemetery also reported from Puthi-Seman, Bedwa-2 and Bhaini Bharo.

15 BHAINI SURJAN-3 (76°15'45"N, 29°10'10"E)
There is another ancient site in the jurisdiction of the village. This site is located about 5 km west of the village and about 200 m east of the Jui canal. It is located about 200 m east of the Bhaini Surjan Minor Head. This site is located on sand-dunes of about 3 m in height. The eastern part of the site has been totally removed during the construction of the Bhaini Surjan Minor. The site occupies an area of about 1.4 ha, totally under cultivation. It has yielded remains of the Mature and Late Harappan periods. A few full-size bricks of the ratio 1:2:4 were also collected during the exploration. The ceramic evidence recovered from the site is similar to those from Bedwa-2.

BHIANI MATOO

This village is lies about 5 km northwest of the Meham town and a road bifurcating from the Meham-Seman Road leads to the village.

16 BHIANI MATOO-1 (76°14'05"N, 29°08'20"E)
About 1 km southeast of the village is an ancient mound which measures about 1.7 ha. The southern and western parts of the mound have been completely removed. The remaining part is about 1.2 m high from the surrounding ground level. On this mound sherds of Late Harappan pottery, stamped pottery of Early Historical period and Medieval pottery were found. Some fragments of faience bangles were also found during the exploration.

BHAINI BHARO

The village Bhaini Bharo is about 5 km southwest of the Meham town and a road bifurcating from NH no.10 leads to this village. There are two ancient mounds in the jurisdiction of the village.

17 BHAINI-BHARO-1 (76°14'40"N, 29°04'35"E)
This ancient mound lies about 1 km west of the village on the left side of the Bhaini Bharo-Sukhpura Road. The site is located in the foot of high sand-dunes. The owner of the land is Shri Tara, s/o Shri Koshar (Nana). This site is totally under cultivation and spread over an area of about 2.2 ha. Due to the levelling for cultivation the site has been reduced to the surrounding ground level. The ceramic evidence recovered during the exploration belongs to the Historical and Medieval periods.

Figure 9 Bhaini Surjan-1 General view

Figure 10 Bhaini Surjan-1 General view

18 BHAINI BHARO-2 (76°13'50"N, 29°04'30"E)

The archaeological site Bhaini Bharo-2 lies about 500 m west of the village. This site falls in the *panchyati* land. It occupies an area of about 2 ha and about 1.5 m high from the surrounding field level. This site is totally under cultivation. The PGW and associated red ware along with Medieval pottery can easily picked up from this site. This is a new site which is being placed on the map for the first time.

19 BHAINI BHARO-3

The archaeological site Bhaini Bharo-3 lies about 5 km southwest of the village. This site falls in the revenue of two villages, i.e Bhaini Bharo and Dhanaa (Bhiwani District). The Bhaini Bahro-Dhanaa Road passes through the site. This site is located on sand-dunes. The potsherds are found over an area of about 1 ha. The ceramic evidence found here is similar to those from Bedwa-2, i.e. the late phase of the Mature Harappan or the early Late Harappan periods. During the course of levelling the site, a number of bones and human skull was also found, indicating that there was a cemetery on this site. This type of cemetery is also reported from Puthi-Seman (Hisar District), Bedwa-2, etc.

BHARAN

The village Bharan is situated at a distance of about 20 km east of the Meham town and about the same distance west of Rohtak. An approaching road from the Madina village leads to this village. There are two ancient sites of archaeological importance in the revenue area of the village.

20 BHARAN-1 (76°27'25"N, 29°04'50"E)

The site of Bharan-1 (Figure 11) lies about 1.5 km north of the village and about 500 m on the left side of the Bharan-Nindana Road. This site falls in the fields of Shri Driya Singh, s/o Shri Shankar Lal. It occupies an area of about 2 ha and has been almost reduced to the surrounding ground level by cultivation. The ceramic industry represented on the mound is the Late Harappan pottery. Two beads of steatite and a few fragments of faience bangles recovered during the exploration. This site was initially discovered by Surender Singh (1989: 17).

21 BHARAN-2 (76°27'45"N, 29°05'00"E)

There is another site about 1.5 km north of the village and about 300 m on the right side of the Bharan-Nindana Road. It spreads over an area of about 2 ha and is about 1 m high from the surrounding ground level. The whole site has been levelled down to the surrounding ground level for cultivation purpose. The owner of the land is Shri Ramphal, s/o Shri Bhagwan. The ceramic industries represented on the site belong to the PGW period. The common shapes include dishes, bowls, basins in the GW, jars, vases, handmade pots and basins in the associated red ware. The antiquities found at the site includes terracotta discs and *ghata*-shaped bead, etc.

FARMANA

The village Farmana lies about 14 km north of the Meham town. This village is situated on the Meham-Julana Road. There are five ancient sites in the jurisdiction of the village.

22 Farmana-1 (76°20'05"N, 29°11'05"E)

This site (Figure 12) is about 4 km west of the village on the left side of the Farmana-Seman Road. This site is locally known as Daksha Khera. This site falls in the revenue jurisdiction of three villages, viz. Farmana, Seman and Bhaini Chanderpal. Major portion of this site falls in the village of Farmana so the author include this site in Farmana.

This site was reported by Dr. Suraj Bhan for the first time, but he did not give details about its location and size. He reported that he found the Early-Siswal (Early Harappan) remains (Suraj Bhan 1974:125).

Figure 11 Bharan-1 General view

Later, Surender Singh gave more details about the site. He estimated the size of the site about 250 m × 250 m and reported pre-/Early Harappan, Mature Harappan, Late Harappan including OCP and Early Historic remains (Surender Singh 1989: 17).

The total area of this site is about 15 ha and rises to a height of about 3 m. The whole site is under cultivation. Farmana-1 is quite big in size and qualifies to be termed as a town or a small city. The location of this site is also very important because this is about 25 km away from the Rakhigarhi. According to Dr. Manmohan Kumar this type of settlements are 'primary type' (Manmohan Kumar *et al.* 2004-05: 26).

During the exploration bichrome pottery and chocolate slip ware, some shards with graffiti marks of Early Harappan period, Harappan pottery, Late Harappan pottery, PGW and Early Historical pottery were found. In addition, Dr. Manmohan Kumar found some sherds of the Hakra Ware from this site (Manmohan Kumar 2005-06: 197). Besides pottery, the antiquities recovered from this site are a complete spearhead of copper, beads of agate, lapis lazuli, carnelian, faience, steatite and terracotta. Chert blades and cores, copper rods, terracotta hubbed wheel, fragments of toy cart frame, bull figurine, terracotta cakes of triangular, '8'-Shaped, *idli*-shapes and faience and terracotta bangles of the Harappan period were also found.

23 FARMANA-2 (76°23'15"N, 29°11'35"E)

This site is within the area of the village and partially under occupation. It measures 2 ha and is about 4 m high from the surrounding ground level. The site was initially discovered by Surender Singh (Surender Singh 1989: 18) who reported medieval remains here. The present author also found the same remains and collected a large number of glass bangles.

24 FARMANA-3 (76°21'15"N, 29°13'03"E)

Another archaeological site is located in the revenue

Figure 12 Farmana-1 General view

Figure 13 Farmana-3 General view

area of the village at a distance of 1.5 km on the Farmana-Bedwa Road (Figure 13). This site is locally known as Girori Khera. The most of this site has been levelled down by the villagers for an agriculture purpose. This site occupies an area of 8 ha and about 2 m high from the surrounding ground level. Dr. Suraj Bhan reported the Late Siswal type pottery on Farmana-3 (Suraj Bhan 1974: 125). But in the absence of any detail, it is quite difficult to say whether he wrote about this site or some another one. The later exploration reported Medieval pottery from this site.

During the course of the exploration by the present author, a few sherds of Early, Mature and Late Harappan periods, some Kushana and Medieval pottery were also found. Besides pottery, the present author recovered a graffiti mark on a sherd, terracotta *idli*-shaped cakes, triangular cake and a fragment of '8'-shaped cake. Two coins of the Yaudheys were also recovered during the exploration, which can be dated to c. second - third century ACE.

25 FARMANA-4 (76°21'40"N, 29°14'30"E)

This archaeological site is located about 2 km northwest of the village. A *kaccha* road from the Bedwa-Farmana Road leads to the site. This entire site occupying an area of about 2.65 ha is under cultivation. The height of the mound is almost the same as that of the surrounding ground level. The owner of the land is Shri Sandeep, s/o Shri Chander. The only ceramic industry represented on the site is the Late Harappan pottery. The main shapes collected from the site include dishes with a drooping rim, bowls, basins, jars with collared rim, deep dishes and miniature pots. Besides the pottery, fragments of faience bangles and terracotta cakes are the main finds from the site.

26 FARMANA-5 (76°24'25"N, 29°13'40"E)

Another archaeological site of Farmana lies about 1.5 km northeast of the village and about 300 m east of Farmana-Dorad Road. The owner of the land is Dr. Harsvroop Boora, Ex. M.L.A. This site has been levelled down to the surrounding ground level and is presently used for the cultivation. The potsherds are found over an area of 1.6 ha. This site is locally known as Boora-ali-Kanger. During the exploration the site yielded GW including a few painted sherds, coarse red ware, red slipped ware and tiny sherds of glazed ware. Based on the above-mentioned evidence, it can be suggested that the site was occupied during the PGW and Medieval periods.

GANGANAGAR

The village Ganganagar is about 9 km east of the village. An approaching road from a new bus stand in Meham leads to the village. This is the smallest village in the Meham Block. There are two ancient mounds in the revenue area of the village.

27 GANGANAGAR-1 (76°23'45"N, 29°05'05"E)

The site Ganganagar-1 is located about 400 m southwest of the village and about 300 m south of Ganganagar-2, and a *pakka* cart track leads towards the site. This site is locally known as Dariyapur Khera. It occupies an area of 2.5 ha and is now 1.5 m high. Some part of the mound is used for a residential purpose and the rest of the site is under cultivation. On the whole mound, sherds of the Late Harappan pottery, PGW and associated red ware were found (Figure 14). Some fragments of faience bangles were also found during the exploration.

28 GANGANAGAR-2 (76°23'47"N, 29°05'07"E)

There is another site in the jurisdiction of this village which is about 300 m southwest of the village. This site spreads over an area of about 1 ha and as low as the ground level. A modern Samsan Ghat or crematory is located at this site, while the rest of the site is under cultivation. Sherds of the PGW. along with associated red ware are found here. The main shapes collected from the site are dishes, bowls, basins, vases, etc.

Figure 14 Ganganagar-1 General view

GIRAWAD

The village Girawad is 22 km northeast of the Meham town and about the same distance from Rohtak. A road bifurcating from NH no.10 at the Madina village leads to this village. There are two archaeological sites located within the revenue area of the village.

29 GIRAWAD-1 (76°33'20"N, 29°07'05"E)

About half a kilometer south of the village, the site of Girawad-1 is located (Figure 15). The Madina-Girawad Road passes through the site. The whole site is now levelled down to the surrounding ground level and is used for an agriculture purpose. This site spreads over an area of 1.3 ha. This site yielded evidence of Late Harappan and PGW periods. This site was earlier explored by Surender Singh who reported only PGW remains (Surender Singh 1989: 19). Late Harappan remains were found by the present researcher. The main shapes in the pottery are jars with collared rim, dish-on-stand, vases, basins, etc., of the Late Harappan period and bowls, dishes, basins, etc., of the PGW.

30 GIRAWAD-2 (76°35'15"N, 29°07'30"E)

About 2 km east of the village, there is a mound. The Girawad-Samargopalpur Road passes through the site. It occupies an area of about 4 ha and about 1 m high from the surrounding field level. It falls in a barren land. The eastern and southern parts of the site has been levelled down for an agriculture purpose. Some portion of the site has been removed for constructing the Girawad-Samargopalpur Road.

The culture represented at the site are the pre-Harappan or Hakra Culture, and Early, Mature and Late Harappan cultures. Some circular structures are visible on the surface. A wall of mud bricks with the typical Harappan ratio 1:2:4, about 1.8 m wide was visible up to the length of 6 m. This wall which runs just in the middle of the site divides the site into two

Figure 15 Girawad-1 General view

parts.

Bichrome sherds were also recovered during the exploration. Besides pottery a good number of antiquities were also recovered from this site. A gold ornament of 2 g in weight and a gold object of 3 cm in length along witl, a copper arrowhead, a copper chisel, a fragment of copper fish-hook and many other unidentified copper objects were found. Another notable discovery from the site was 20 steatite beads. A large quantity of copper objects indicates that this site must have been an industrial site. In the course of levelling the ground, the villager found a silver coin hoard of the Sultanate period. The present author obtained only one specimen for photograph.

KHARKHRA

The village Kharkhra is about 7 km east of the Meham town. On the NH no.10, it is about 23 km west of Rohtak. Within the revenue jurisdiction of the village, there are two sites of archaeological importance. Both the sites were discovered by Surender Singh (Surender Singh 1989: 19-20).

31 KHARKHRA-1 (76°26'40"N, 29°02'20"E)

This site (Figure 16) lies about 300 m southwest of the village. The owner of the land is Shri Tek Ram, s/o Shri Badlu Ram. This site is locally known as Khera. It occupies an area of 2 ha and is as low as the surrounding ground level. The western part of the site is occupied by the modern habitation, which is about 1 m high. The sherds of Late Harappan pottery, PGW and Early Historical pottery were found on the site. A terracotta bull figurine of the PGW period and fragments of faience bangle are among the antiquities found from the site.

32 KHARKHRA-2 (76°27'15"N, 29°01'45"E)

This site is located about 1 km south of the village. It measures about 3 ha in size and presently used for an

Figure 16 Kharkhra-1 General view

agriculture purpose. During the exploration, sherds of red ware and red slipped ware were found. The main shapes are incurved-rim bowls, vases, lids, spouted vases and carinated *handis*. Earlier Surender Singh reported a few Kushana coins from the site (Surender Singh 1989: 20, pl. III). On the basis of the amove-mentioned evidence, it can be suggested that the site was occupied during the Kushana and Gupta period.

KHERI MEHAM

The village Kheri Meham is about 500 m north of Meham town. There are many medieval monuments in the village. Especially this village is popular for its Sati memorials. There is only one site in the revenue jurisdiction of the village.

33 KHERI MEHAM-1 (76°22'10"N, 29°06'55"E)

This site is located about 200 m north of the village. This falls in the *panchayati* land. It occupies an area of about 2.7 ha and it is now 1 m high from the surrounding ground level. The whole site is under cultivation. It has yielded remains of the pre-Harappan or Hakra Culture, Early Harappan Culture, Mature Harappan, Late Harappan, Historical and Medieval periods. This site is very rich in material remains. Faience bangles were found in a large quantity. This gives an idea that this site must have been a faience production site where beads and bangles were manufactured. Other antiquities include terracotta cake of different shapes, i.e. triangular, circular, *idli*-shape, and *mustikas*, terracotta bangles, terracotta biconical beads and hubbed wheel, etc. Apart of these, agate, carnelian, steatite beads were discovered. A complete Harappan basin was found on the site. Mr. Deepak of the same village recovered fragments of a large storage jar from the site and he is kind enough to provide it to the present author.

MADINA

The village Madina is 15 km east of the Meham town and about the same distance from Rohtak on NH no.10. There are seven ancient sites within the revenue jurisdiction of the village.

34 MADINA-1 (76°30'15"N, 29°04'02"E)

This site lies about 1.5 km west of the village adjacent to the Mokhra Minor and about 200 m southeast from where the Mokhra minor starts. At present this site is partially occupied by the Bhoot Nath temple, while the rest of the area is under cultivation. The site occupies an area about 1 ha. The author found a few sherds of Late Harappan pottery from this site. This site was initially discovered by Surender Singh (1989: 20).

35 MADINA-2 (76°30'05"N, 29°02'55"E)

This site is located about a distance of 2 km southwest of the village. A cart track from the village leads to the site. It occupies an area of about 3 ha and about 3 m high from the surrounding ground level. The owners of the land are Shri Anand Singh Dangi, s/o Shri Ami Lal, and Shri Jugti Ram, s/o Shri Miwu. This site is locally known as Khera. Mr. Anand Singh Dangi, M.L.A. and Ex. min ster, owns some complete bowls of the PGW period and he was kind enough to let me photograph these (Pl. 16). The ceramic industries represented on the site are Late Harappan pottery, PGW, BSW and Early Historical pottery. Besides the pottery, a very fine etched carnelilen bead, two copper arrowhead, *ghata*-shaped bead, faience bangles, sling ball, terracotta disc, etc., were found. This site was initially discovered by Surender Singh (1989: 20).

36 MADINA-3 (76°30'10"N, 29°01'50"E)

The site Madina-3 (Figure 17) is located about 3 km southwest of the village on the left side of the Mokhra minor. The owner of the land is Shri Dayanand, s/o Bhagwan Ram. This site is locally known as Khera. Most of the site is levelled down to the surrounding ground level for an agriculture purpose. The southern part on the mound is still intact. This is about 2 m high from the ground level and occupies an area of about 2 ha. The PGW and BSW can easily be picked from this site. A pestle of black stone was found during the exploration. This site was initially discovered by Surender Singh (1989: 20).

37 MADINA-4 (76°33'55"N, 29°33'20"E)

This site lies about 2 km west of the village and is about 400 m north of NH no.10. The Shital Baba Temple Road passes through the site. The owner of the fields is Shri Chand, s/o Shri Dayanand. Locally this site is known as Khera. This site is located on sand-dunes, which are about 5 m high and spread over an area about 2 ha. Surender Singh reported only Medieval pottery on this site (Surender Singh 1889: 21). The present author discovered a Kushana coin hoard from the site. This hoard contains 68 coins. Some typical Kushana bricks were also seen at the site. In addition, some sherds of stamped pottery of Historical and Medieval periods were also found.

38 MADINA-5 (76°30'50"N, 29°33'45"E)

The fifth site (Figure 18) is about 2.5 km east of the village and is about 800 m north of a radio station. A *kaccha* road from the Shital Baba temple road leads to the site. The geography of the site is very interesting. This site is situated on very high sand-dunes about 8 m high. This site spread over an area of 1.7 ha. It has yielded evidence of the late Mature Harappan or the early Late Harappan periods. The pottery recovered from the site is akin to those from Bedwa-2.

39 MADINA-6 (76°30'02"N, 29°03'25"E)

This site is about 1.5 km west of the village and is about 500m south of NH no.10. This site is about 500 m north of Madina-2. The site is totally under cultivation. It occupies an area of about 1.5 ha. The site has yielded the GW including some painted

Figure 17 Madina-3 General view

Figure 18 Madina-5 General view

sherds, BSW, coarse red ware, and the main shapes are bowls, dishes, basins in the GW and storage jars, vases, hand made basins, etc., in red ware. On the basis of the above-mentioned evidence, it can be suggested that the site was occupied during the PGW period.

40 MADINA-7 (76°32'30"N, 29°05'30"E)

This site is located about 2 km north of the village. The Madina-Girawad Road passes through the site and divides it in two parts. This site is in about 2 ha in size and levelled down for cultivation. The PGW and Early Historical pottery were found during the exploration. The main shapes include bowls and dishes of PGW, and stamped jars, vases, lipped bowls of the Historical period.

MEHAM

The Meham town is about 28 km west of district head quarter Rohtak on NH no.10 and is a tehsil head quarter. References to Meham are seen in *Mahabharata*. In *Mahabharata,* it is referred that Nakul, a Pandava warrior, conquered ten forts in the west of Khandava-Parastha. Mitittna (Meham) was one of them (*Mahabharata* II: 29), which is situated to the west of Rohitiki (Rohtak) the capital of the Yaudheya republic. This place can be identified with the modern Meham town. There are four ancient sites within the revenue jurisdiction of the town. The sites, Meham-1, Meham-2 and Meham-3 were initially discovered by Surender Singh (1989: 22).

41 MEHAM-1

This site of Meham-1 (Figures 19 and 20) is totally occupied by the modern habitation of the Meham town. It spread over an area of about 50 ha and about 15 m high from the surrounding ground level. Some sherds of Late Harappan, PGW, Historical and Medieval pottery were collected from the exposed sections and gullies formed at the mound. Three stone sculpture of early Medieval period reported earlier from Meham-1 (Shila Devi 1975: pl.XXX-E).

42 MEHAM-2 (76°20'15"N, 29°24'50"E)

The extent of the site is about 2 ha and about 1 m high from the surrounding gtound level. As this site falls within the compound of the Government College, Meham, a considerable part of the mound has been removed by the people to build college building. The ceramic industry represented on the site is Medieval pottery, the main shapes including jars, vases, bowls, spouted pots, etc. Some sherds of Glazed Ware were also collected.

43 MEHAM-3 (76°19'45"N, 29°24'30"E)

The third archeological site of Meham is located to south of the town close to a baoli of the Mughal period. Locally this site is known as Khera. It occupies an area of about 1 ha. It has yielded Medieval pottery which has common shapes like sharp-edge bowls, channel pots, lids without side knob, vases, basins, etc. The antiquities found here are fragments of glass bangles.

44 MEHAM-4 (76°35'15"N, 29°07'30"E)

There is yet another site about 2 km southwest of the town. This site lies on the left side of the Meham-Bhaini Bharo Road and about 50 m east of the Late Shri Jogi Ram samadhi. The owner of the land is Dr. Amar Singh, s/o Shri Jogi Ram. The site is about 2.3 ha in size and has been levelled down to the surrounding ground level due to the removal of the soil. All over the site, sherds of PGW, Historical and Medieval pottery are encountered. The pottery of the PGW period include bowls and dishes. Main shapes of the Historical period are incurved-rim bowls, jars, basins, sherds with stamped designs, etc., while the Medieval pottery has knife-edge bowls, lids with rope design, jars and vases.

Figure 19 Meham Medieval structure

Figure 20 Meham-1 Habitational mound

MOKHRA

The village Mokhra is about 20 km east of the Meham town and about the same distance, west of Rohtak. A road bifurcating from Madina on NH no.10 leads to the village. There are five archaeological sites in the revenue area of the village.

45 MOKHRA-1 (76°28'50"N, 28°58'30"E)

This site is located about 2 km northwest of the village in the common land of the village and is close to a pond that is locally known as Rojh-ala-Dabada. It measures about 2 ha in size and almost as low as the ground level. The ceramic industry represented on the site is Medieval pottery only. The site was initially discovered by Surender Singh (1989: 23). Common shapes found here are small dishes, bowls, jars, knobbed lids and channel-spouted pots, etc. The antiquites found from the site are fragments of glass bangles.

46 MOKHRA-2 (76°29'10"N, 29°59'40"E)

This site is located about 2 km northwest of the village in the common land of the village. This site is close to a pond that is locally known as Karne-ali-Bani. Most of the site has been removed for cultivation. It occupies an area of about 2 ha and rises to a height of 2 m. Suriender Singh reported PGW and Medieval pottery from this site (Surender Singh 1989: 23). The present author discovered Late Harrapan remains from the site. Late Harappan pottery includes dishes, dish-on-stand, basins, jars with collared rim, etc., while the PGW consists mainly of bowls and dishes.

47 MOKHRA-3 (76°28'30"N, 29°01'09"E)

This archaeological site lies about 5 km west of the village on the Mokhra-Kharkhra Road. This area is locally known T.B. (Tuberculosis) since the local villagers compare this barren land due to salt with disease. This site falls in the common land of the village. It occupies an area of about 2 ha and is now 0.5 m high from the surrounding ground level. Completely the site has been removed during the construction of the Mokhra-Kharkhra Road. The ceramic industries represented on the site are the Early and Late Harappan pottery, and the PGW. Among the antiquities are a few fragments of faience and terracotta bangles and undefined copper objects.

48 MOKHRA-4 (76°27'30"N, 28°59'30"E)

This site is about 4 km southwest of the village. A *kaccha* track from the Mokhra-Bassana Road on the left side of the Bassana Minor leads to the site. The owner of the land is Shri Kala, s/o Munshi. The whole site is under cultivation and has been reduced to the ground level. The potsherds spread over an area of about 2 ha. During the exploration, the site yielded red ware and red polished ware with the main shapes of vases, carinated *handis*, incurved-rim bowls, jars, etc. On the basis of shapes and surface treatment of the above-mentioned ceramic industries, the site may be placed under the Kushana and Gupta period.

49 MOKHRA-5 (76°32'40"N, 29°00'40"E)

This site is about 3 km northeast of the village and about 1 km south of a radio station (Madina). This site is locally known as Kholu-ala-Khera. This site falls in the revenue jurisdiction of two villages, Madina and Mokhra. The site falls equally in both the villages but since the site is near to Mokhra than Madina, the present author includes this site in Mokhra. This site measures 2 ha and is about 2 m high from the surrounding field level. The PGW and associated red ware can easily be picked up from this site. Some sherds of the Late Harappan period were also found during exploration. This is a new site placed on the archaeological map.

NIDANA

The viilage Nidana is about 23 km west of the Meham town and about 25 km west of Rohtak. A road, bifurcating from NH no.10 near Madina, leads to the village. There are three sites of archaeological importance within the jurisdiction of the village.

50 NIDANA-1 (76°35'03"N, 29°04'55"E)
This archaeological site is located at the point where the Nidana-Girawad Road and the Nidana-Madina Road meet. The site falls in the *panchayati* land of the village. Some part of the site is occupied by modern habitation. The village primary health centre is also situated on the site, while the rest of the site is under cultivation. This site measures about 1 ha in size and as low as the surrounding ground level. The ceramic industry represented here is only the Medieval pottery (Surender Singh 1989: 23).

51 NIDANA-2 (76°35'10"N, 29°04'50"E)
About 300 m further west of the above-mentioned mound (Nidana-1), there lies another mound which measures 2.5 ha and it is now 3 m high. At present the site is no longer intact, as the whole mound of the site has been removed and is under cultivation. All over the mound, sherds of Historical and Medieval pottery are found (Surender Singh 1989: 24).

52 NIDANA-3
The archaeological site of Nidana-3 is located about 1.5 km west of the village and is about 300 m east of a drain. This site is situated on sand-dunes of about 1 m high, spreading over an area of about 1 ha. It has yielded evidence of the late Mature Harappan or the early Late Harappan periods. The main shapes include dish-on-stands, pedestalled vases, vases, storage jars, bowls, etc. The pottery recovered from the site is akin to those from Bedwa-2.

NINDANA

The village Nindana is about 8 km north of the Meham town on the Meham-Gohana Road. There are seven sites of archaeological importance in the revenue jurisdiction of the village.

53 NINDANA-1 (76°44'50"N, 29°08'30"E)
The site Nindana-1 is located about 2 km west of the village on the Sajanwala Johda cart-track. The owners of the land are Shri Surta Ram, s/o Shri Molar Ram, and Shri Hari Chand, s/o Shri Bharthu Ram. This site spreads over an area about 2 ha and is as low as the surrounding ground level in height. The ceramic industries represented on the site are PGW, Historical and Medieval pottery. This site was initially discovered by Surender Singh (1989: 24).

54 NINDANA-2 (76°25'20"N, 29°08'50"E)
This site is located about 2 km northwest of the village. The Nindana-Seman Road passes through the site. The owner of the land is Shri Jitu Ram, s/o Jawahara Ram. The site spreads over an area of about 2 ha and is about 1 m high from the surrounding ground level. The northern and western parts of the site are under cultivation. The rest of the site has been disturbed by the extractors of saltpetre. The sherds found on the site are of Medieval pottery only.

55 NINDANA-3 (76°27'40"N, 29°08'15"E)
This site is about 3 km east of the village. The area on which this site lies is locally known as Bhani-ala-Kehat and the site is locally called as Khera. It measures about 2.7 ha and is about 2.5 m high. The site has been disturbed by the extractors of saltpetre. The ceramic industry represented on the site is Medieval pottery only.

56 NINDANA-4 (76°27'20"N, 29°07'40"E)
Another site within the revenue jurisdiction of the Nindana village is located about 2 km east of the village. The area where this site lies is locally known as Bhani-ala-Kehat. It measures about 1.5 ha and is about 1.5 m high from the surrounding ground level. The whole site is under cultivation. The ceramic industry represented on the site belongs to Medieval times.

The main shapes include sharp-edged-rim bowls, jars, basins, knobbed lids, *handis* and storage jars, etc.

57 NINDANA-5 (76°24'30"N, 29°08'55"E)

The Nindana-5 is located about 1 km south of the village and about 1 km west of the Meham-Gohana Road. This site measures about 1.2 ha and is as low as the surrounding ground level. The entire site is under cultivation. The owner of the land is Pandit Satbir, s/o Shri Lakshman. It has yielded the remains of Medieval period. The antiquites found from this site include glass bangles of black and blue in colour.

58 NINDANA-6 (76°25'10"N, 29°07'10")

The archaeological site of Nindana-6 is located about 2 km south of the village and about 800 m east of the Meham-Gohana Road. The owner of the land is Shri Ram Diya, s/o Shri Surta Singh. The entire site is under cultivation. It has yielded evidence of Historical and Medieval periods.

59 NINDANA-7 (76°25'20"N, 29°07'20"E)

The archaeological site of Nindana-7 is located about 2 km south of the village and about 800 m east of the Meham-Gohana Road and about 200 m north of Nindana-6. The owner of the land is Shri Partap Namberdar, s/o Shri Shawak Ram. This site is locally known as Khaghal-ala-Khera. The eastern and northern parts of the site are under cultivation. This site spreads over an area of about 2 ha and about 2 m high from the surrounding fields. The PGW and associated red ware can easily picked up from this site. Besides these, it has also yielded evidence of Historical and Medieval periods.

SEMAN

The village Seman (Figure 21) is situated at a distance of about 8 km north of the Meham town and a road from Farmana leads to this village. There are six ancient sites in the revenue jurisdiction of this village.

60 SEMAN-1 (76°19'50"N, 29°11'10"E)

Seman-1 (Figure 22) is located about 2 km east of the village and about 200 m south of the Seman-Farmana Road. The owner of the land is Shri Hardewa Ram, s/o Shri Ram Kala. It occupies an area of about 2.5 ha and about 2 m high from the surrounding ground level. Some part of the site is in Farmana. During the exploration the site yielded evidence of the Early, Mature and Late Harappan periods. Terracotta cakes of triangular, *mustika*, circular and *idli*-shape, terracotta hubbed wheels and bangles, beads of steatite and faience, faience bangles, stone balls, etc., are among the antiquities found from the site.

61 SEMAN-2 (76°19'10"N, 29°11'15"E)

This archaeological site is located about 2 km east of the village and about 800 m southwest of Seman-1. The owner of the land is Shri Bhale Ram, s/o Shri Dhanpat. It measures about 2 ha and about 2 m high from the surrounding ground level. The whole site is under cultivation and is located on sand-dunes. The ceramic industry represented on the site is Medieval pottery. This site was initially discovered by Surender Singh (1989: 26).

62 SEMAN-3 (76°18'05"N, 29°11'40"E)

Another site of the village which is named as Seman-3 is located about 1.2 km east of the village on sand-dunes. A *kaccha* track leading to Sukhawala-Jodh passes through the site. The site spreads over an area of about 1.3 ha and is totally under cultivation. This site has yielded evidence of the Late Harappan period, which is similar to those from Bedwa-2. The main shapes include dish-on-stands with flaring rim and rib below the junction between the dish and stand, bowls, vases with under-cut rim, goblets with ring-base, pedestalled vases, etc.

63 SEMAN-4 (76°17'50"N, 29°11'35"E)

This site of Seman-4 is located about 1 km east of the village and is surrounded by sand-dunes all around.

Figure 21 Seman Medieval temple

Figure 22 Seman-5 General view

A *kaccha* road to Sukhawala-Jodh passes through the site. It occupies an area of about 1 ha. The whole site is under cultivation. The ceramic industry represented on the site belongs to the Historical and Medieval periods. The main shapes of the Historical pottery include incurved-rim bowls, jars, basins, etc., while the Medieval pottery includes knife-edged-rim bowls, pots, jars, *handis*, etc. A good number of glass bangle pieces of the Medieval period were also collected in the course of exploration.

64 SEMAN-5 (76°16'10"N, 29°11'50"E)

Another site in the village called Khera is located at a distance of about 200 m southwest of the village behind the Sahid Jashvir Singh Samarak. This site falls in the *panchayati* land. It measures about 1.80 ha. All over the mound, sherds of the Late Harappan, PGW, Historical and Medieval periods are found. The Late Harappan pottery includes jars, storage jars with collared rim, dishes, etc. The PGW consists of bowls and basins of medium to fine fabric. The Historical and Medieval pottery include jars, basins, bowls, lids, etc., as common shapes. The antiquities collected from the site are terracotta and faience bangles, steatite beads and some undefined copper objects.

65 SEMAN-6 (76°17'40"N, 29°13'50"E)

This site is located about 5 km northwest of the village and about 300 m south of the Bedwa-Puthi Road. It is located on sand-dunes of about 5 m in height. This site is about 300 m south of the burial site at Puthi-2. The whole site has been levelled down for cultivation. It measures about 2 ha. It has yielded pottery which is exactly the same as those from Bedwa-2.

SEKHPUR TITRI

The Sekhpur Titri village is situated about 5 km east of the Meham town. An approachable road from the Meham bus stand leads to the village. There is an archaeological site in the revenue area of this village.

66 SEKHPUR TITARI (76°24'20"N, 29°05'30"E)

This site is located to the north of the modern habitation. This site is locally known as Titari-Khera. It occupies an area of about 2.5 ha and about 1 m high from the surrounding field levels. While the northern portion of the site is under cultivation, the rest of the site is unoccupied. The ceramic industry represented on the site belongs to the Late Harappan, Historical and Medieval periods. The antiquities collected from the site include bangle pieces of faience and a steatite bead. This site was initially discovered by Surender Singh (1989: 26).

SISAR KHAS

The Sisar Khas village is located about 5 km to the south of the Meham town. There are two ancient sites in the revenue area of the village.

67 SISAR KHAS-1 (76°15'10"N, 29°01'20"E)

The archaeological site of Sisar Khas-1 lies at a distance of 3 km west of the village and about 50 m south of the Sisar-Badesara Road. The owner of the land is Shri Amar Singh, s/o Shri Ami Lal. This site is locally known as Khera. This site spreads over an area of about 2 ha and as low as the surrounding ground level. The ceramic industry represented at the site belongs to the Historical and Medieval periods.

68 SISHAR KHAS-2 (76°15'50"N, 29°01'15"E)

This archaeological site is located about 1.5 km southwest of the village near the foot of sand-dunes. The whole site is under cultivation and occupies an area of about 1.2 ha and about 2 m high from the surrounding ground level. The owner of the land is Shri Dayand, s/o Shri Puran Khati. This site has yielded remains of the Late Harappan period. The pottery recovered from the site is akin to those from Bedwa-2.

CHAPTER III

SETTLEMENT PATTERN

Settlement pattern as a subject of study has drawn the attention of many scholars from different scientific disciplines like geography, sociology, archaeology, etc. Research on settlement pattern is to be carried out in the context of varying ethnological, historical and geographical facts. While the present work is primarily based on the available archaeological data, a substantial help has been taken from ethnography and geography. This chapter deals with the settlement pattern of the Meham Block during the Proto-Historic, Historical and Medieval periods. The data gathered in the exploration have been utilized to reconstruct the settlement pattern.

The ecological, cultural and social patterns of the ancient people are reconstructed by archaeologists from the remains discovered from surface and from excavation. An archaeologist derives his knowledge of an ecological system from geography and sociology. Thus archaeology and sociology are two disciplines for the reconstruction of the ways of life of people in the ancient times. Social and cultural activities of people are distributed over landscapes. The manner in which the activities including cultural, social and ecological system are distributed is known as settlement pattern.

The concept of settlement pattern was applied to archaeological remains as a byproduct of close relationships between ethnographers and archaeologists and this new discipline is known as settlement archaeology. But unlike ethnographers and geographers, archaeologists are unable to recover an entire settlement pattern, as only the physical remains are found as archaeological remains (Rouse 1972: 96). Scholars have tried to interpret the term of settlement pattern in their own respective ways.

Gordon Willey was one of the first scholars who wrote on settlement pattern. He defines the term of settlement pattern as the way in which the human beings disposed themself over the landscape on which they lived. Settlement pattern refers to the arrangement of dwellings, the nature and disposition of building pertaining to community life, etc. These patterns are influenced by the natural environment, the level of technology of the people and the interaction of social and cultural institutions. As the settlement patterns are determined by the cultural needs, they offer a crucial point for the functional interpretation of archaeological remains (Willey 1953: 1). In other context, Willey compared settlement pattern with the settlement arrangements reflecting the adjustment of man and culture to the environment and to the social organization (Willey 1956: 1).

Willey has used the settlement pattern approach for the study of structures and functioning of specific past societies. But there are others whose interpretations for the term vary considerably. The K.C. Chang's differentiation of two meanings of settlement pattern is pertinent. According to him, settlement pattern, strictly defined, means the manner in which human settlement are arranged over the landscape in relation to physiography and environment. Another meaning is the community pattern referring to the manner in which the inhabitants arranged their various structures within the community and the way the communities are arranged in the "aggregate" which means a gathering of a certain number of communities bound by the social, political, military, commercial or religious conditions (Chang 1958: 229).

William T. Sanders gave a broad definition of

settlement pattern. According to him, the study of settlement pattern is a study of the ecological and demographic aspects of a culture. He equates the settlement pattern with the distribution of population over landscape and investigation of the reasons behind the distribution (Sanders 1956: 105).

According to B. Trigger, "The settlement pattern is an expression of the societal aspects of ancient cultures. The study of change in settlement falters thus becomes the study of the development of social and political organization" (Trigger 1965: 2).

S.J. Kundson views the settlement pattern as "that unit which is created when a group of human being occupies a particular geographical region to exploit its resources. The resulting distribution of the sites is what most archaeologists refer to as a settlement pattern" (Kundson 1978: 61).

SETTLEMENT ARCHAEOLOGY

An archaeological study of settlement pattern is the focal point of a new theme of study called "settlement archaeology". Its proper connotation was first given by G.R. Willey. He applied the concept of settlement archaeology and settlement pattern to interpret archaeological data. He however said that there is no settlement approach to archaeology. Settlement archaeology extends the ambit of archaeological study. In settlement archaeology, two schools of thought have developed. In one school, regarded as old school of thought, a settlement has a purely locatory connotation of artefacts and tangible remains in localities showing evidence of domestic activity. The other school, called the new school, defines settlement archaeology as a study of social relationships using archaeological data and not as an analysis of archaeological settlement. Although archaeologists agree that an analysis of settlement archaeology is a crucial category for understanding human behaviour, there are multifarious approaches to the study itself. Trigger suggested that settlement should be studied at three levels, viz. (a) individual building, (b) settlement layout which is equivalent to community layout, (c) settlement distribution or the spatial relationships between different communities of a zonal scale (Trigger 1967: 151).

The different factors to be studied in an analysis of settlement pattern have been summarized by R. Tringham (1972: 18) as follows.

(a) Location of the settlements and their relation to the ecology, the natural resources and system of communication.
(b) Density and distribution of the settlements.
(c) Distribution of specialized activity loci, viz. burial sites, butchering sites, etc.
(d) Distribution of population.
(e) System of trade between settlements and distribution of markets.
(f) Differential exploitation of the same gross ecological zone, e.g. pastoral, rural, urban, etc.

COMPARATIVE METHOD

A very fruitful method of study of settlements patterns is the comparative method. This is done by careful comparison of the archaeological remains in sites with the corresponding elements of excavated sites and with contemporary habitation. In India, the different stages of progress in the cultural evolutionary process are found to exist at different geographical locations at the same time. For example, coexistence of highly complex urbanized societies in cities and towns of a country with tribes and clans in the interior pockets of the same country, who are even now at the stages of hunting, gathering and pastoral life, shifting cultivation and semi-urban can be seen. The coexistence of these different phases of life helps an investigator to reconstruct the lives of the past settlements.

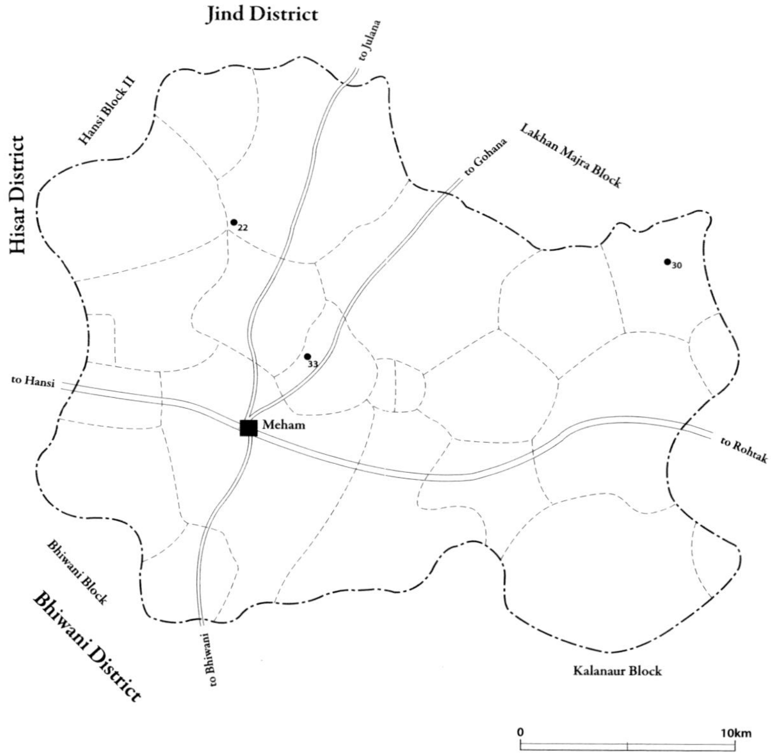

Figure 23 Distribution of pre-Harappan or Hakra Culture sites

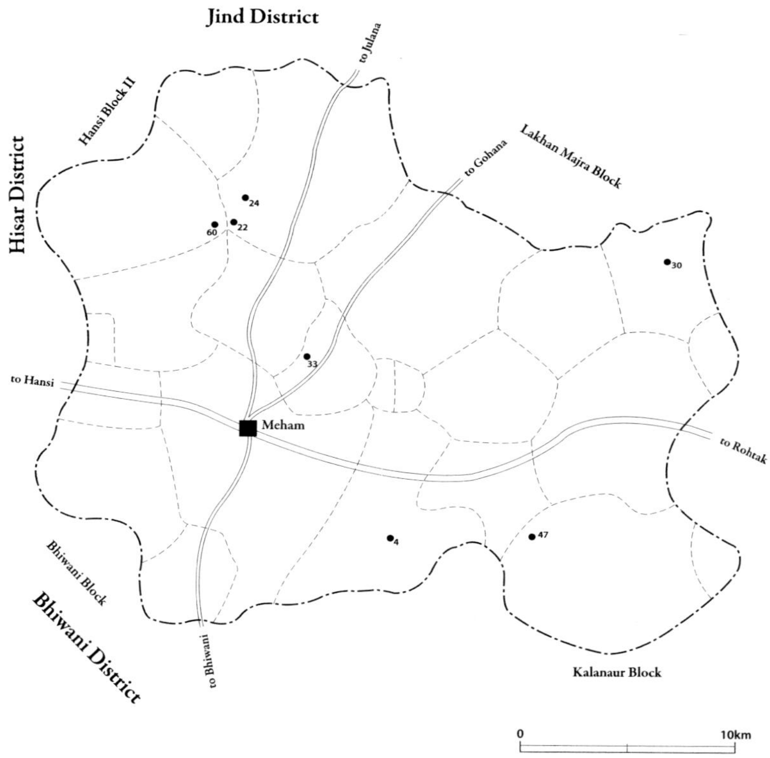

Figure 24 Distribution of Early Harappan sites

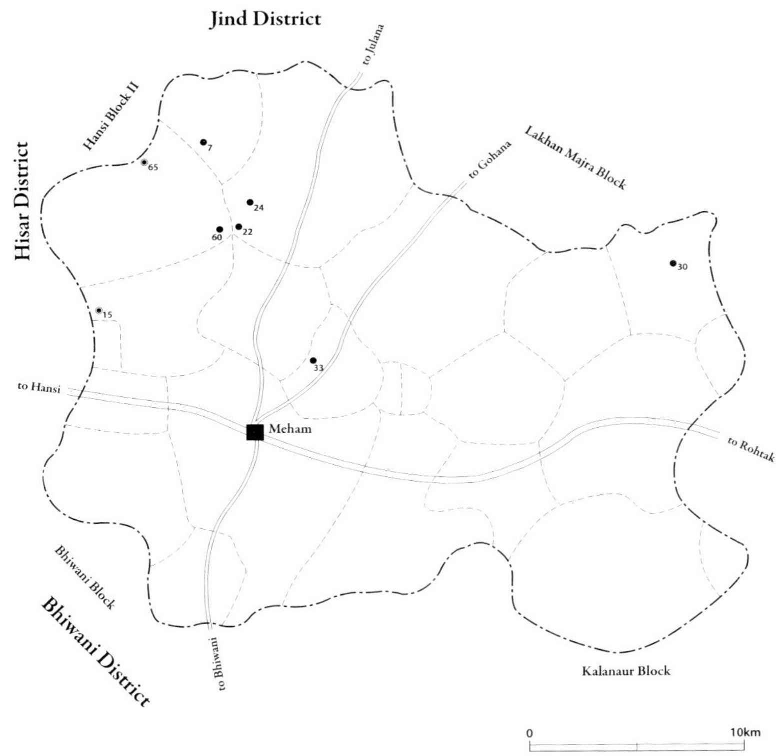

Figure 25 Distribution of Mature Harappan sites

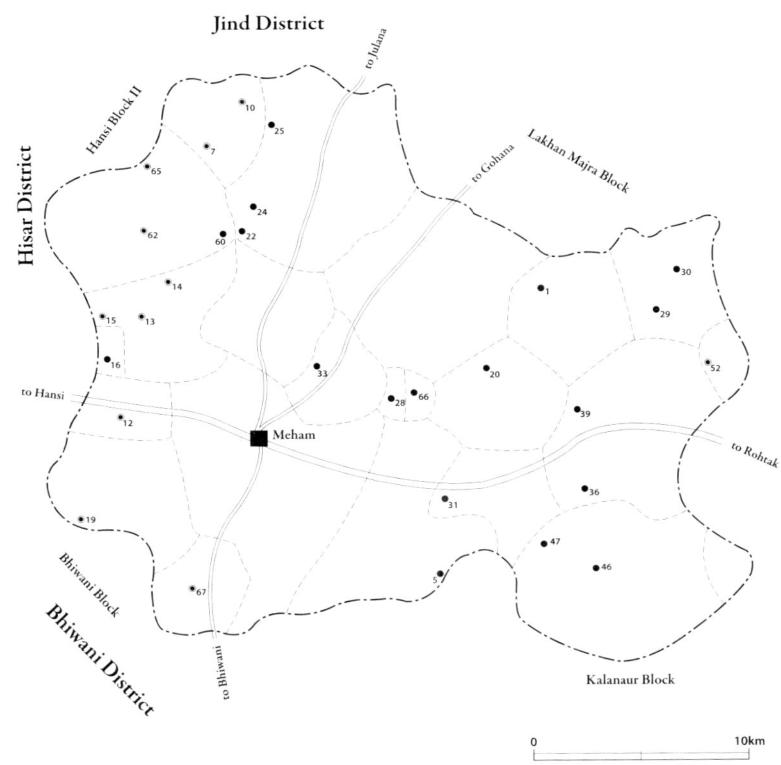

Figure 26 Distribution of Late Harappan sites

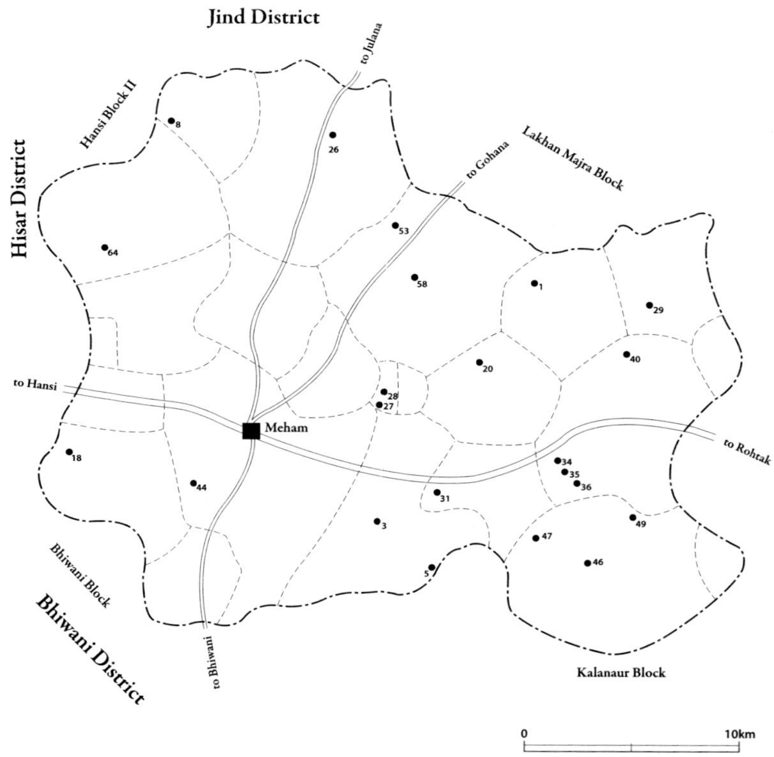

Figure 27 Distribution of PGW sites

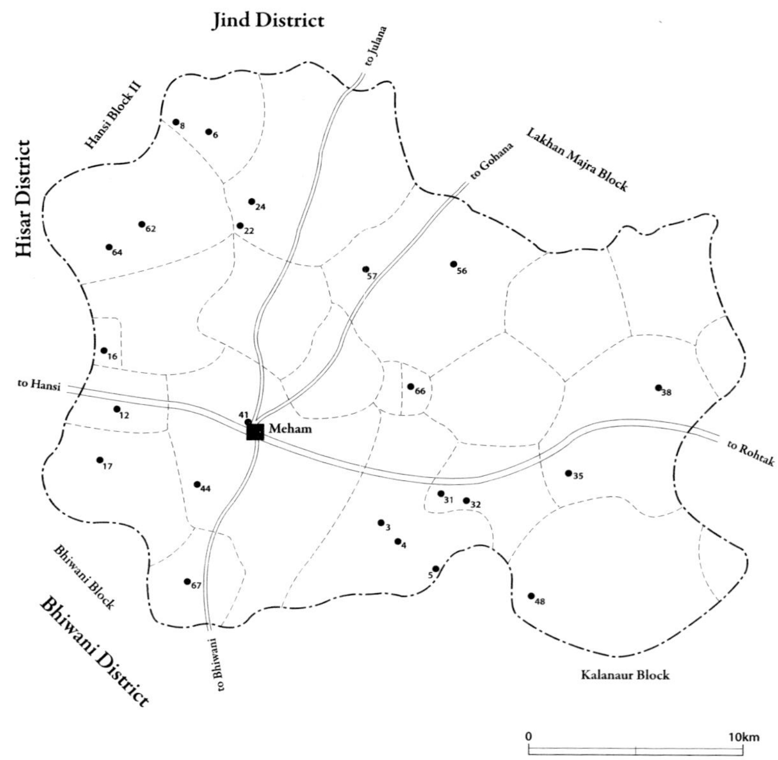

Figure 28 Distribution of Early Historical and Historical sites

Table 1 Number of sites during different cultural periods

Culture period	Alluvial plain	Sandy area	Total
Early Harappan	7	1	8
Malure Harappan	5	2	7
Late Harappan	18	12	30
PGW	22	0	0
Historical	20	3	23
Medieval	29	8	37

Table 2 Number of sites in respect of size during different cultural periods

Culture Period	Size (ha)	Alluvial plain	Sandy area	Total
Early Harappan	1-1.99	1	1	2
	2-2.99	2	-	2
	3-3.99	1	-	1
	4-4.99	1	-	1
	5-5.99	-	-	-
	6-6.99	-	-	-
	7-7.99	-	-	-
	8-8.99	1	-	1
	9-	1	-	1
	Total	7	1	8
Mature Harappan	1-1.99	0	1	1
	2-2.99	2	1	3
	3-3.99	-	-	-
	4-4.99	1	-	1
	5-5.99	-	-	-
	6-6.99	-	-	-
	7-7.99	-	-	-
	8-8.99	1	-	1
	9-	1	-	1
	Total	5	2	7
Late Harappan	1-1.99	4	7	11
	2-2.99	8	4	12
	3-3.99	1	-	1
	4-4.99	2	-	2
	5-5.99	-	1	1
	6-6.99	1	-	1
	7-7.99	-	-	-
	8-8.99	1	-	1
	9-	1	-	1
	Total	18	12	30
PGW	1-1.99	5	-	5
	2-2.99	12	-	12
	3-3.99	3	-	3
	4-4.99	1	-	1
	5-5.99	-	-	-
	6-6.99	1	-	1
	Total	22	-	22
Historical	1-1.99	2	2	4
	2-2.99	12	-	12
	3-3.99	-	-	-
	4-4.99	2	1	3
	5-5.99	-	-	-
	6-6.99	1	-	1
	7-7.99	-	-	-
	8-8.99	1	-	1
	9-	2	-	2
	Total	20	3	23

Culture Period	Size (ha)	Alluvial plain	Sandy area	Total
Medieval	1-1.99	7	2	9
	2-2.99	17	3	20
	3-3.99	-	-	-
	4-4.99	1	1	2
	5-5.99	-	2	2
	6-6.99	1	-	1
	7-7.99	-	-	-
	8-8.99	1	-	1
	9-	2	-	2
	Total	29	8	37

SCOPE AND LIMITATION OF PRESENT CHAPTER

In the present chapter, the present author has tried to study through the Trigger's third level of settlement pattern studies, i.e. the zonal pattern. The author has been unable to study the first and second levels, as detailed data on the internal structures of sites are not available. The main body of data for this chapter comes from the author's fieldwork in the Meham Block, the Rohtak District.

The periods which suggest the maximum occupation and population during successive cultures are as follows.

Pre-Harappan	4500 BCE to 3000 BCE
Early Harappan	3000 BCE to 2500 BCE
Mature Harappan	2500 BCE to 1750 BCE
Late Harappan	1750 BCE to 1500 BCE
PGW	1200 BCE to 600 BCE
Medieval	1206 ACE to 1707 ACE

LIMITATION

There were several limitations for the reconstruction of the settlement pattern in the area of the present study. It is rather difficult to say that the total number of sites discovered is exactly the same as that of the settlements occupied during the periods. The size of sites during different cultural periods has been decided on the basis of the area in which specific pottery spread over. It is also difficult to determine whether a site was temporarily or permanently occupied or the whole site was occupied in a given period or only for a small portion of time.

SIZE AND DISTRIBUTION OF SETTLEMENT

This part of the chapter deals with the distribution pattern of sites in general with respect of their size. The earliest culture identified in the area of present study is the pre-Harappan culture which recently tends to be called as the Hakra Ware culture by several archaeologists. The total number of the pre-Harappan sites in Meham is three, viz. Farmana-1, Girawad-2 and Kheri Meham. With respect to size, Farmana-1 is about 15 ha, Girawad-2 about 4 ha and Kheri Meham about 2.7 ha. Farmana-1 is the only site having an area of more than 5 ha. It is not possible to say that the earliest farming culture that occupied the site was actually occupying the whole site or not. It is quite possible that they occupied a small portion of the existing sites and the succeeding cultures were responsible for the expansion of the site.

There are total eight Early Harappan sites, viz. Bedwa-2, Farmana-1, Farmana-2, Seman-1, Kheri Meham, Girawad-2, Bahelba-2 and Mokhra-3, of which seven sites are located in the alluvial plain and one is located on the sandy area. With respect to the

Table 3 Total number of sites and area occupied by each category of sites

Cultural Period	Size of sites	Alluvial plain		Sandy area		Total	
		No. of sites	Area occupied	No. of sites	Area occupied	No. of sites	Area occupied
Early Harappan	1-1.99 hect	1	1	1	1.5	2	2.5
	2-2.99 hect	2	5.2	-	-	2	5.2
	3-3.99 hect	1	3	-	-	1	3
	4-4.99 hect	1	4	-	-	1	4
	5-.99 hect	-	-	-	-	-	-
	6-6.99 hect	-	-	-	-	-	-
	7-7.99 hect	-	-	-	-	-	-
	8-8.99 hect	1	8	-	-	1	8
	Above 9 hect.	1	15	-	-	1	15
	Total	7	36.2	1	1.5	8	37.7
Mature Harappan	1-1.99 hect	-	-	1	1.5	1	1.5
	2-2.99 hect	2	5.2	1	2	3	7.2
	3-3.99 hect	-	-	-	-	-	-
	4-4.99 hect	1	4	-	-	1	4
	5-.99 hect	-	-	-	-	-	-
	6-6.99 hect	-	-	-	-	-	-
	7-7.99 hect	-	-	-	-	-	-
	8-8.99 hect	1	8	-	-	1	8
	Above 9 hect.	1	15	-	-	1	15
	Total	5	32.2	2	3.5	8	31.7
Late Harappan	1-1.99 hect	4	5.67	7	9.2	11	14.87
	2-2.99 hect	8	17.7	4	8	12	25.7
	3-3.99 hect	1	3	-	-	1	3
	4-4.99 hect	2	8.8	-	-	2	8.8
	5-.99 hect	-	-	1	5	1	5
	6-6.99 hect	1	6.5	-	-	1	6.5
	7-7.99 hect	-	-	-	-	-	-
	8-8.99 hect	1	8	-	-	1	8
	Above 9 hect.	1	15	-	-	1	15
	Total	18	64.67	12	22.2	30	86.87
PGW	1-1.99 hect	5	7.2	-	-	5	7.2
	2-2.99 hect	12	24.9	-	-	12	24.9
	3-3.99 hect	3	9.5	-	-	3	9.5
	4-4.99 hect	1	4.8	-	-	1	4.8
	5-.99 hect	-	-	-	-	-	-
	6-6.99 hect	1	6.5	-	-	1	6.5
	Total	22	52.9	-	-	22	52.9
Historical	1-1.99 hect	2	32	2	2.5	4	5.7
	2-2.99 hect	12	26.2	-	-	12	26.2
	3-3.99 hect	-	-	-	-	-	-
	4-4.99 hect	2	8.8	1	4	3	12.8
	5-.99 hect	-	-	-	-	-	-
	6-6.99 hect	1	6.5	-	-	1	6.5
	7-7.99 hect	-	-	-	-	-	-
	8-8.99 hect	1	8	-	-	1	8
	Above 9 hect.	2	65	-	-	2	75
	Total	20	127.7	3	6.5	23	134.2
Medieval	1-1.99 hect	7	10.3	2	2.5	9	12.8
	2-2.99 hect	17	37.1	3	6.2	20	43.3
	3-3.99 hect	-	-	-	-	-	-
	4-4.99 hect	1	4	1	4	2	8
	5-.99 hect	-	-	2	10	2	10
	6-6.99 hect	1	6.5	-	-	1	6.5
	7-7.99 hect	-	-	-	-	-	-
	8-8.99 hect	1	0.8	-	-	1	8
	Above 9 hect.	2	75	-	-	2	75
	Total	29	140.9	08	22.7	37	163.6

Table 4 Mean settlement size during different cultural periods

Cultural Period	Alluvial plain (ha)	Sandy area (ha)	Total (ha)
Early Harappan	5.12	1.5	4.71
Matue Harappan	6.44	1.75	5.10
Lafe Harappan	3.59	1.85	2.89
PGW	2.40	-	-
Historical	6.38	2.16	5.83
Medieval	4.85	2.83	4.42

Table 5 Number of settlements of different categories in the Meham Block

Culture Period	Urban centre	Small town	Big village	Small village
Early Harappam	-	1	1	6
Mature Harappam	-	1	1	5
Late Harappam	-	1	2	27
PGW	-	-	1	21
Historical	1	1	2	19
Medieval	1	1	2	33

Table 6 Average population per km^2 during different cultural periods

Cultural Periods	Alluvial Plain	Sandy Area	Average
Early Harappan	5.13	0.21	5.34
Mature Harappan	4.56	0.49	5.06
Late Harappan	9.16	3.14	12.31
PGW	7.49	-	7.49
Historical	18.1	0.92	19.02
Medieval	19.97	3.21	23.87

Table 7 Mean population per settlement during different cultural periods

Culture Period	Alluvial Plain	Sandy Area	Total
Early Harappan	307.14	89.0	279.8
Malure Harappan	382.6	104.0	303
Late Harappan	213.38	109.9	172
PGW	142.81	-	142.8
Historical	379.25	128.66	346.56
Medieval	288.62	168.5	268.64

size-wise distribution, there are two sites in the 1.0-1.99 ha category, two sites in the 2.0-2.99 ha category, one site in the 3.0-3.99 ha category, one site in the 4.0-4.99 ha category and one site respectively in the 8.0-8.99 ha and above 9 ha categories. The total floor area occupied during this period was 37.7 ha. Of this, 36.2 ha is in the alluvial plain and 1.5 ha in the sandy area (Table 3). The mean size of settlements in the whole Meham is 3.33 ha (Table 4).

There are seven sites of the Mature Harappan period. Among these, five sites are located in the alluvial plain and two sites are located on the sandy area. In the category of 1.0-1.99 ha there is only one site, which is located in the sandy area. In the category of 2.0-2.99 ha, there are two sites in the alluvial plain. In the categories of 3.0-3.99 ha and 4.0-4.99 ha, there is only one site respectively. The latter one is located in the alluvial plain. In the categories of 8.0-8.99 ha and above 9.0 ha, there is only one site respectively and both are located in the alluvial plain (Table 2). The total floor occupied during the Mature Harappan period is 35.7 ha, of which 32.2 ha is in the alluvial plain and 3.5 ha in the sandy area (Table 3). The mean size of settlements in the whole Meham is 4.095 ha during this period (Table 4).

The number of sites during the Late Harappan period is 30, of these 18 are in alluvial plain and 12 in sandy area. Of these settlements, the number of sites below 2 ha is 11. In 2.0-2.99 ha category, there are 12 sites and 3.0-3.99 hect there is only one site. In the category 4.0-4.99 ha, there are two sites. In the categories of 6.0-6.99 ha, 8.0-8.9 ha and above 9.0 ha, there is only one site in each. The total floor area occupied during the Late Haprappan period is 86.87 ha, of which 64.67 ha is in the alluvial plain and 22.2 ha on the sandy area (Table 3). The mean size of settlements in the whole Meham Block during this period was 2.72 ha. The mean size in the alluvial plain is 3.59 ha and that in the sandy area is 1.85 ha (Table 4). The highest number of sites (12) falls in the category of 2.0-2.99 ha, followed by sites (11) below 2.0 ha. Thus, of the 30 sites, 23 are below 3.0 ha (Table 3).

The total number of PGW sites is 22, all of which are located in the alluvial plain. In respect of size, five of them are below 2 ha. In the 2.0-2.99 ha category, there are 12 sites. In the 3.0-3.99 hect. size there are three sites. In the 5.0-5.99 and above 6.0 ha categories, there is only one site in each class. The total floor area which are occupied during the PGW period is 52.9 ha (Table 3). The mean size of the settlements in the whole Meham Block is 2.4 ha (Table 4).

Of the Historical period there are 23 sites, of which 20 sites are located in the alluvial plain and three sites in the sandy area. In the category of below 2.0 ha there are four sites and in the category of 2.0-2.99 ha, there are 12 sites. In the 4.0-4.99 ha category there are three sites. In the categories of 6.0-6.99 ha and 8.0-8.99 ha, there is one site in each. In the category of above 9.0 ha, there are two sites. The pattern of site development shows that a majority of the settlements is small in size as among these 23 settlements 16 sites remain below 3.0 ha. The total floor area occupied during this period is 134.2 ha. Of this 127.7 ha was in the alluvial plain and 6.5 ha in the sandy area. The mean size of settlements for the whole Meham Block is 4.27 ha (Table 3). The mean size of sites in the alluvial plain is 6.38 ha and that in the sandy area is 2.16 ha (Table 4).

The number of sites during the Medieval period is 37, of which 29 sites are located in the alluvial plain and eight sites in the sandy area. Of these settlements, the number of sites below 2.0 ha is 9 and in the category of 2.0-2.99 ha, it is 20. In the 4.0-4.99 ha and 5.0-5.99 ha categories there are two sites in each. In the 6.0-6.99 ha and 8.0-8.99 ha categories there is only one site respectively. There are two sites of above 9.0 ha (Table 3). The total habitational area of 29 sites in the alluvial plain is 140.9 ha, while the total area of eight sites in the sandy area is only 22.7 ha (Table 3). The mean size of settlements is 3.84 ha in Meham as a whole. The mean size of sites is 4.85 ha in the alluvial plain and that in the sandy area is 2.83 ha (Table 4). The highest number of sites, 20 in number, falls in the category of 2.0-2.99 ha, followed by sites, nine in number, of below 2 ha. Thus, of the 37 sites, 29 are below 3 ha in size. (Table 3).

SIZE AND SPACING OF SETTLEMENTS

In the previous section, we have seen that there is a distinct relationship between ecological factors and distribution of settlements of different sizes. If the rank-size rule – the number of settlements of a given type continue to increase as the size decreases – was to operate, then we should expect the spacing of settlements to be gravened mainly by their size (Brush and Bracy 1955: 599-69). Large settlements are widely spaced. The rank-size rule in the spacing of settlements operates only in the case of settlements of the same size (Haggellet *et al.* 1977: 128). However, as Thomas (1961) points out, this does not necessarily mean that the population of the sample settlements and the neighbour settlements are exactly of the same size, rather these are "approximately the same size". It means that if we attempt to estimate the spacing pattern of the settlements, we have to evolve a site typology, a classification that reflects difference in size, function, structures and other attributes of sites of the same period.

J.R. Parson (1971: 18) and R.E. Blanton (1972: 58) in their studies of the settlement patterns in the Mexico valley classified sites into a number of categories on the basis of population, which is as follows:

Primary regional center	over 2000 persons
Secondary regional center	between 1000 and 2000 persons
Nucleated villagebetween	100-1000 persons
Hamlet	10-100 persons

In the South Asian context, Allchin and Allchin (1997: 156-7) have categorized the Harappan sites in the four grades, viz. grade one (100-200 hectares), grade second (10-15 ha), third grade (5-10 ha) and grade four (1-5 ha). But their generalization cannot hold ground for all the regions of the Harappan sphere as the different geographical areas have different characteristics, which determine site setting, their size and functional vistas. Mughal has conducted extensive archaeological explorations in Cholistan and has formulated his concept of the hierarchy of settlements (Mughal 1997: 55-56). In the present study the present researcher have adopted his classification. Manmohan Kumar also follows the same classification (Manmohan Kumar 2009) which is as follows.

Size	*Nature of Settlement*
0.1-5 ha	Small village
5.1-10 ha	Big village
10.1-20 ha	Small town
20.1-30 ha	Big town
30.1-40 ha	Small city
More than 40 ha	Large city

The size-wise categorization of the sites in the Meham Block are as follows (Table 5).

Out of eight Early Harappan sites, six sites have area of less than 5 ha and thus fall in the categories of small village. Only one site falls in the category of big village. While only one site falls in the category of small town.

During the Mature Harappan period, of seven settlements, there were five small villages and one big village, while only one site falls in the class of small town.

During the Late Harappan period of 30 settlements, there are 27 small villages, two big villages and only one small town.

During the PGW period, of 22 settlements, only one site can be classified as big village, while the rest is

Table 8 Estimate of population in the Meham Block during different cultural periods

Cultural Periods	Population in Alluvial Plain	Population in Sandy Area	Total Population
Early Harappan	2150 (96.02%)	89 (3.97%)	2239
Mature Harappan	1913 (90.19%)	208 (9.80%)	2121
Late Harappan	3841 (74.43%)	1319 (25.56%)	5160
PGW	3142 (100%)	-	3142
Historical	7585 (95.15)	386 (4.85%)	7971
Medieval	8370 (86.12%)	1348 (13.87%)	9718

considered as small village.

During the Historical period, of 23 settlements, 19 were small villages, two big villages, one small town and one is large city.

During the Medieval period, of 37 settlements, 33 settlements were small villages, two big villages, one small town and one urban center.

POPULATION

The population estimates of the archaeological sites in the Meham Block is based on the habitational area of the sites and compared with the modern settlement areas and population of the Meham Block (Tables 6-8). An accurate population estimate of a site is of great interest but the factors affecting population size within a given area are so numerous that the accurate estimate of population and density is difficult though not impossible. The size of settlement, structures found in excavation, demographic observation on contemporary settlements and mathematical models given by demographers are the means for estimating the past population.

In the present study the total floor area is used for the estimation of population. The estimates are obviously very tentative. Due to various limitations, a better demographic estimate can be made only where the total settlement has been laid bare to show the layout of structures and the relationship of different structure within it. Unfortunately in the area of present study, not a single site has been excavated. In the absence of excavation data, we have to depend upon the exhaustive exploration of sites and contemporary settlements and households. In 1961 there are 59.40 persons per ha^2 in Haryana (Statistical Abstract of Haryana 1971-72) According to my calculation, this figure fits for the estimates for the population of different settlements.

During the Early Harappan period the total estimated population of the Meham Block is 2239, of which 2150 persons live at seven sites in the alluvial plan and 89 at one site in the sandy area. The average population is 5.34 per km^2 in the block. The average population per settlement is 279.8 persons.

During the Harappan period the total estimated population is 2121, of which 1913 (90.19 %) are distributed over five sites and 208 (9.80 %) are distributed on two sites in the sandy area. In the category between 500-1500 persons, there was only one site and there are three sites respectively in the categories of 150-500 persons and below 150 persons. The density is 5.06 persons per km^2. The average population per settlement is 303 persons.

During the Late Harappan period, the total estimated population is 5160, of which 3841 (74.43 %) are distributed over 18 sites in the alluvial plan and 1339 (25.5 %) are distributed over 12 sites in the sandy area. A large number of population is estimated to have lived in small villages. The average population per km^2 in the whole Meham is 12.31 person per km^2. The average population per settlement is 172 persons.

During the PGW period, the total number of

estimated population is 3142 at 22 sites which are all located in the alluvial plan in the block as a whole and the population density is 7.49 persons per km^2. The average population per settlement is 142.8 persons.

During the Historical period, the total estimated population is 7971, of which 7585 (95.15 %) is distributed over 20 sites and 386 (4.85 %) is distributed in three sites in the sandy area. Average population of the Meham Block during the Historical period is 19.02 persons per km^2. The average population per settlement is 346. 56 persons.

During the Medieval period, the total estimated population is 9718, of which 8370 (86.12 %) is distributed over 29 sites in the alluvial plain and 1348 (13.87 %) distributed on eight sites in the sandy area. The average population per settlement was 268.84 persons.

CHAPTER IV

STUDY OF POTTERY

Pottery is an important source for the reconstruction of Indian history of those periods to which written records are not available but its importance does not diminishes when written records become available. The study of pottery helps us to reconstruct the daily life of its users. It helps us to correlating it with the social and economic condition. It is generally said that pottery is ABC of archaeology as during the excavation and exploration since potsherds are discovered in most cases. It is one of the aspects of material culture, but it may be regarded that it is the most important key that the archaeologists search may unlock many secrets of the past which would otherwise have remained unknown.

It will be useful to briefly review the characteristic feature and chorological sequence of the ceramics found in the region of the Meham Block of the Rohtak District in order to put the cultural sequence of the Meham Block in a proper perspective. During the course of exploration a huge amount of pottery was collected from the sites in the region of present study which helped us in determining the different cultural periods of ancient sites. The main ceramic industries include pre-Harappan, Early Harappan, Harappan, Late Harappan, Painted Grey Ware (PGW), Early Historical, Historical and Medieval pottery.

The main features of each group are enumerated here. Therefore, a brief description of illustrated potsherds is given according to the above-mentioned cultural sequence. An attempt is also made to compare the potsherds with those from the excavated sites in India.

PRE-HARAPPAN POTTERY

The earliest group of the ceramic industry of this region is the pre-Harappan pottery. A part of pre-Harappan pottery is called 'Hakra Ware' by some archaeologists on the basis of the comparison with those from Cholistan (Khatri and Acharya 1995; Rao *et al.* 2003, 2004, 2005).

M.R. Mughal first reported this type of the pottery from Cholisthan (Mughal 1997). In India this type of pottery was first reported from Kunal as the pottery of the earliest settlers (Khatri and Acharya 1995). This site is about 75 km northwest of Meham. Dr. Amarendra Nath also reported the same type of pottery from Rakhi Garhi (Nath 2001). This type of pottery was also found in abundance at Bhirrana in the context of pit dwelling. The excavator of Bhirrana divided this type of ceramic into eight classes (Rao *et al.* 2004-05: 61-2).

Mud Appliqué Ware

On this type of pottery, a thick coat of mud is applied. In some cases the mud is applied directly on the pot surface. The entire body of the pot is interspersed with white quartz granules. The rims are painted in black with a band. The main shapes are globular pots and storage jars.

Incised Ware

This type of pottery is generally red to bright red in appearance. Pre-firing incisions with a sharpened reed are executed on the exterior from shoulder to belly. The patterns are usually rows of chevrons, criss-crosses, parallel lines and wavy lines. The main shapes are small vases, handled vases and *lota*.

Figure 29 Pre-Harappan Pottery from the Meham Block

Tan Slipped/Chocolate Slipped Ware

This type of pottery is well fired having medium to fine fabric. A thick slip of tan colour is applied to red surface. Main shapes are vase, bowls, etc.

Black Burnished Ware

This type of ceramic is represented by black or grey pottery. The main shapes are squattish pots, bowls, etc.

Brown or Buff Ware

This type of pottery was painted in brown on buff surface.

Bichrome Painted Ware

This type of ceramic, represented by two colour painting, i.e. the painting is executed on the exterior over red slip; the outline of the motifs is executed in black and the inner space is filled with white. The painted motifs are geometric and floral. The shapes encountered in this ware are mainly vases and bowls.

Black-on-Red Ware

On this type of pottery, painting was executed in black on red surface. The painted repertoire is essentially geometric in nature consisting of lines, loops, criss-cross, triangles, etc. The main shapes are vases, bowls and cups.

Red Ware

This type of the pottery is the most common. The main shapes are vase, bowls and cups. All shapes are of medium fabric.

DESCRIPTION OF ILLUSTRATED SPECIMENS

Figure 29

1 Fragment of a vase with a squat rim. A thick coat of mud is applied. The entire body of the pot is interspersed with white quartz granules. From Kheri Meham.

2 Fragment of red ware vase. A thick coat of mud is applied. The whole sherd is interspersed with white quartz granules. From Kheri Meham.

3 Sherd of red ware, incised with wavy lines. From Girawad-2.

4 Sherd of red ware, incised with criss-cross lines. From Kheri Meham.

5 Sherd of red ware, incised with parallel lines, painted with black band horizontally. From Farmana-1.

6 Sherd of handled vase, incised with parallel lines and bordered with wavy incised lines. Painted in black with a horizontal band below belly. From Kheri Meham.

7 Sherd of bichrome ware, painted with a pipal leaf. The outline of the motif is in black and filled with white. From Kheri Meham.

8 Sherd of red ware, incised with wavy lines. From Girawad-2.

9 Sherd of red ware, deeply incised with zigzag lines. From Girawad-2.

10 Sherd of red ware, deeply incised with rows of chevrons and criss-cross lines. From Farmana-1.

11 Sherd of black-burnished ware, deeply incised. From Girawad-2.

12 Sherd of red ware, deeply incised with criss-cross lines. From Kheri Meham.

EARLY HARAPPAN POTTERY

The ceramic assemblage of the Early Harappan period is characterized by bichrome painted ware. The surface is dull red on which the decoration is done in black and white pigments. The latter is however used mainly as a subsidiary colour for adding dots and dashes or for filling in solid blanks in order to heighten the effect of paintings by bringing them in relief. The painted designs include a large number of geometric patterns, such as horizontal bands (sometimes as thick as the height of the neck), loops, wavy lines, concentric arches and meanders, notched motif, row of clots, cross-hatched triangles and semicircles, solid opposed triangles, lenticulars, horizontal and vertical chains, tridents and squares, as well as faunal and floral motifs, such as stag, ibex, peacock, cock, fish, bull head, pipal leaf and other plants. Some pots are decorated with incised patterns like wavy lines and criss-cross designs. While some of medium-sized globular vessels have high pedestals and ring base, others are characterized by a flat base.

Pottery of this period has been divided into six fabrics, i.e. Fabric A to F by B.K. Thapar (*IAR* 1962-63: 20).

Fabric A

Fabric A includes vessels made on a wheel. Comparatively light and thin in section and red to pinkish in colour. Painting is done in black and white pigments. The motifs include semicircular arches, lattices, triangles, row of loops and pipal leaf. Globular vases, bowls and basins characterize the main shapes.

Fabric B

Fabric B vessels were made carefully, generally thrown on a wheel. Comparatively heavy and thick in section and red in colour. The main shape is storage jar, which is slipped up to the shoulder and is rusticated down to the base.

Fabric C

This group includes vessels turned on a fast wheel in a very careful manner and betray sophistication. They are made of very fine clay and slipped smoothly in shades of red and plum or purple red. The main shapes are globular and ovoid vase, straight-sided bowl, dish and dish-on-stand. These shapes are essentially painted in black with designs usually geometric but sometimes combined with naturalistic motifs. The vessels of this fabric may be called deluxe ware.

Fabric D

It is marked by heavy jars, troughs and basins. Some

pots are decorated with sharp ridged incisions of varying patterns on the internal surface and single or multiple rows of crude impressions on the outer surface. The pottery is thick and sturdy and treated with red slip.

Fabric E

This fabric includes vessels slipped with buff as reddish buff solution. The texture is medium. The main shapes are jar, dish, bowl, dish-on-stand, bowl-on-stand, chalice, etc. They are dull red to pink in colour with painting in black pigment interspersed with white. The design motifs are both geometric and naturalistic.

Fabric F

Fabric F includes grey colour pottery of medium fabric. The main shapes are the basin, dish-on-stand, bowl and vase. The decoration includes geometric designs.

Early Harappan pottery has been found from Bedwa-2, Behlba-2, Farmana-1, Farmana-3, Girawad-2, Kheri Meham, Mokhra-3 and Seman-1. All the above-given fabric were recovered during the exploration of the area under present study.

DESCRIPTION OF ILLUSTRATED SPECIMENS

Figure 30

1 Fragment of a bowl-cum-basin, with a ridge on the internal side. It is of medium to coarse fabric and burnt to brick red core. From Bedwa-2.

2 Fragment of a bowl-cum-basin, with an out-turned rim. Painted in black with a band on the rim and loops below the rime on the internal side, over light red slip. From Bedwa-2.

3 Fragment of a bowl. It is of medium to coarse fabric and burnt to red core. Painted with broad black band on neck and shoulder. From Bedwa-2.

4 Fragment of a vase, with an inverted rim, raised neck and tapering shoulder. From Bedwa-2

5 Fragment of a pale red ware. Featureless vase with an out-turned rim and tapring sides. From Bedwa-2.

6 Fragment of a vase, with an out-turned rim, concave neck and tapering shoulder. It is of medium fabric, burnt to brick red core. Painted with black horizontal bands on the rim and neck over a light slip. From Bedwa-2.

7 Fragment of a vase of Fabric C with an out-turned, externally grooved rim, short neck and expanding shoulder. It is of medium to coarse fabric, burnt to brick red core. Painted with three black bands above shoulder. From Bedwa-2.

8 Fragment of a jar with an out-turned rim and rounded body. It is of medium to coarse fabric, burnt to brick red core. Painted on the rim and neck. From Bedwa-2

9 Fragment of a red ware vase with an out-turned, externally collared rim and concave neck. Painted with a black band. From Bedwa-2.

10 Fragment of a vase with an out-turned rim, medium fabric and light red core. Painted in black with a horizontal band. From Bedwa-2.

11 Fragment of a vase with an out-turned rim and high neck. It is medium fabric having light red core. Painted with black horizontal bands on the rim. From Bedwa-2.

12 Fragment of a vase with an out-turned and raised neck. It is of medium fabric. From Bedwa-2.

13 Fragment of a storage jar with a wide mouth and an out-turned beaked rim. It is of medium to coarse fabric, burnt to brick red core. From Bedwa-2.

14 Fragment of a storage jar with an out-curved beaked rim and concave neck. It is of medium to coarse fabric, burnt to brick red core. From Bedwa-2.

15 Fragment of a storage jar with a recurved rim and a trapping shoulder. From Bedwa-2.

16 Fragment of a vase, with an out-turned rim and a globular body. It is of medium coarse fabric, burnt to brick red core. Painted with black horizontal band on rim. From Bedwa-2.

17 Fragment of a vase with short out-turned rim

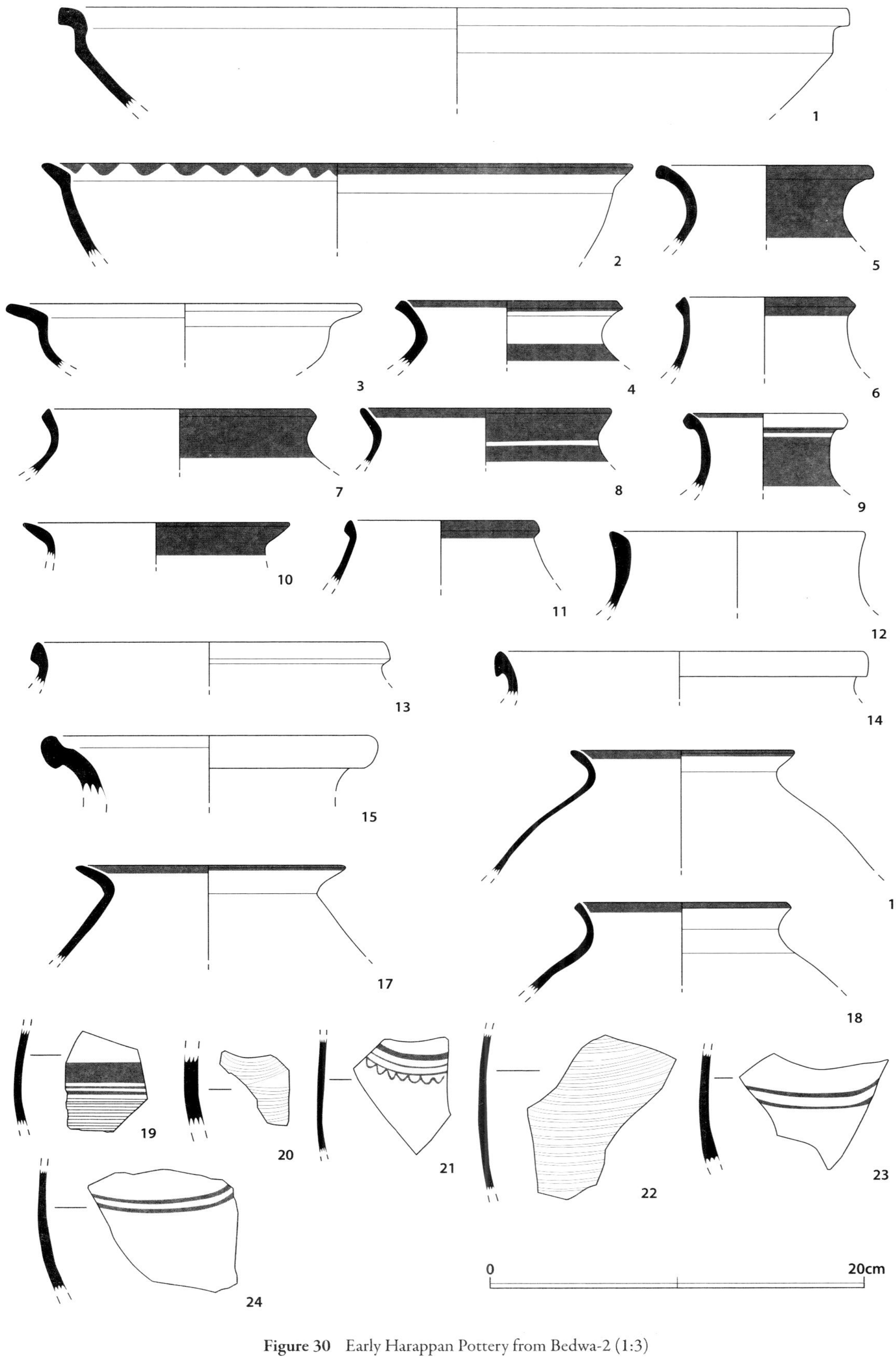

Figure 30 Early Harappan Pottery from Bedwa-2 (1:3)

and rounded body. It is of medium fabric, burnt to brick red core. Painted with black horizontal band on rim. From Bedwa-2.

18 Fragment of a vase with a short, out-turned rim and an expanding shoulder. It is of medium to coarse fabric. From Bedwa-2.

19 Fragment of a vase, painted with black band and incised below the painting. From Bedwa-2.

20 Fragment of a red ware vase, with horizontal zigzag incised lines on the exterior. From Bedwa-2.

21 Sherd of a medium thin red ware, painted in black with three horizontal bands and zigzag line below the bands just touching the band. From Bedwa-2.

22 Sherd of a medium thin red ware, with horizontal incised lines on the exterior. From Bedwa-2.

23 Sherd of a medium thick red ware pained in black horizontal bands. From Bedwa-2.

24 Sherd of a dull ware painted in black with two horizontal bands. From Bedwa-2.

Figure 31

1 Fragment of a storage jar, with a wide mouth and an out-turned rim in convex profile. It is of medium to coarse fabric, burnt to brick red core. A red slip is applied. From Farmana-1.

2 Fragment of a large jar, with a wide mouth and an out-turned rim. It is of medium to coarse fabric, burnt to brick red core. Painted with a black horizontal band on the rim on the external side over a light red slip. From Farmana-1.

3 Fragment of a storage jar, with an out-turned rim.

4 Fragment of a bowl. From Farmana-1.

5 Bowl with an out-turned rim and a tapering side. Painted with two black bands over the lower part of the rim. From Farmana-1.

6 Dish with a short featureless rim and a carinated shoulder. Medium fabric of Fabric F. From Farmana-1.

7 Fragment of a vase with an out-turned rim. Painted with black band above the shoulder. From Farmana-1.

8 Fragment of a vase with an out-everted rim, a raised neck and a tapering shoulder. Painted with black band above the shoulder. From Farmana-1.

9 Fragment of a stem of dish-on-stand of grey ware. It is of fine fabric. From Farmana-1.

10 Fragment of a vase, painted with a band near the shoulder horizontally and zigzag incised lines on the outer side. From Farmana-1.

11 Sherd of a medium thin ware, painted with black horizontal bands and enclosing loops. From Farmana-1.

12 Fragment of a bowl of Fabric D, decorated with zigzag incised lines. From Farmana-1.

13 Fragment of a dish, with a projected rim and a carinated shoulder. From Farmana-1.

Figure 32

1 Fragment of a vase of Fabric C, with an out-turned rim, a concave neck and a tapering shoulder. It is of medium fabric, burnt to red core. Painted with black horizontal bands on the rim and shoulder.

2 Fragment of a vase of Fabric C, with a flaring rim and an ovoid body. It is of medium to coarse fabric, burnt to brick red core. Painted with black band around the rim, neck and shoulder. From Farmana-1.

3 Fragment of a vase of Fabric F with an everted rim and a tapering shoulder. It is of medium fabric and burnt to grey core and surface. From Farmana-3.

4 Fragment of a jar, with an out-turned beaked rim and convex profile. It is of medium to coarse fabric, burnt to brick red core, having a graffiti mark. From Kheri Meham.

5 Sherd of a medium thin red ware, painted in black with two bands associated with concentric arches in the reserved slip manner. From Girawad-2.

6 Sherd of a medium thick red ware, painted in black with loops over dull red exterior. From Farmana-1.

7 Sherd of Fabric C, painted with black band having a graffiti mark. From Farmana-3.

8 Sherd of a medium thin red ware, painted in

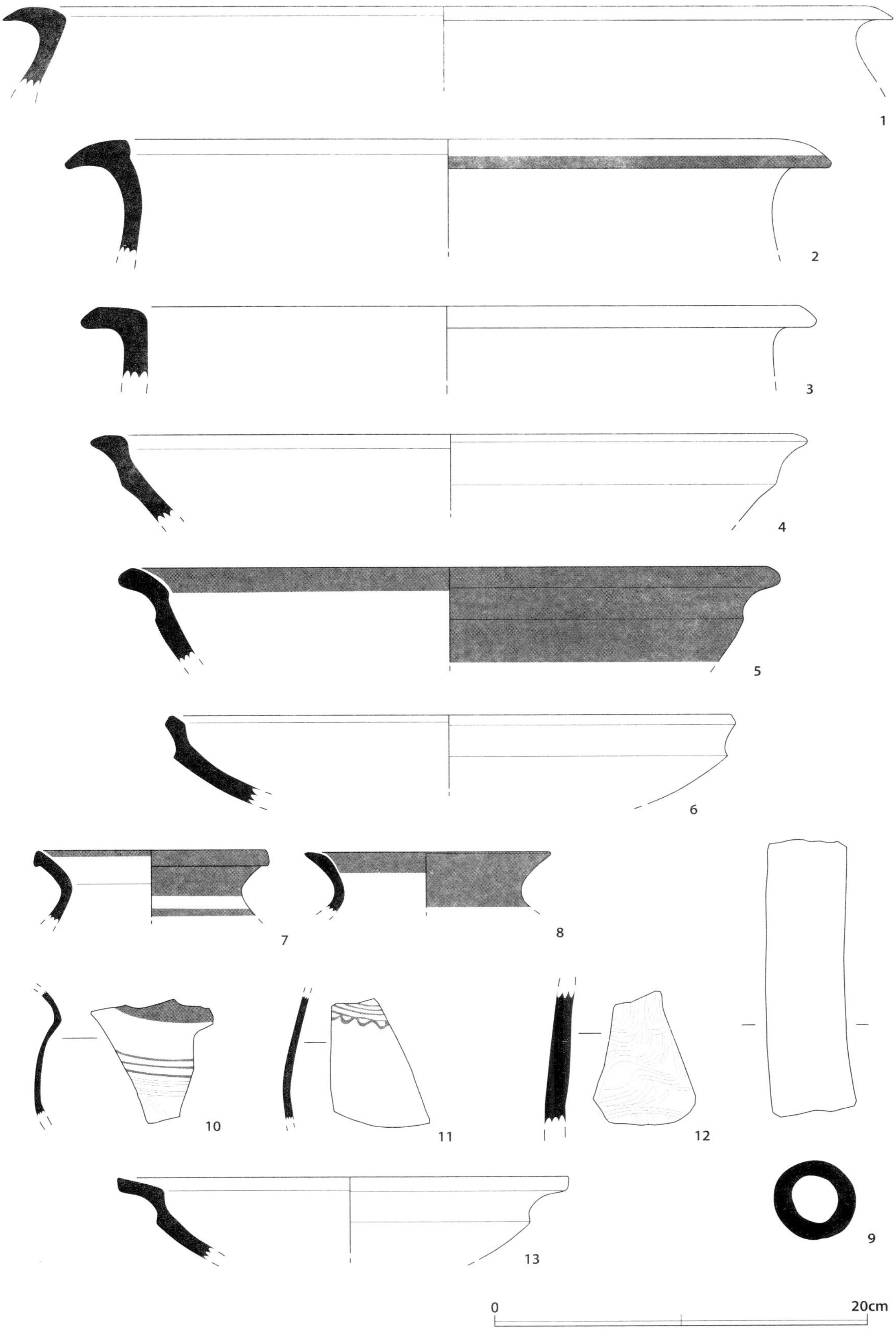

Figure 31 Early Harappan pottery from Farmana-1 (1:3)

Figure 32 Early Harappan pottery from the Meham Block

black with a band and concentric arches. From Kheri Meham.

9 Sherd of Fabric A, painted in black and white with a pipal leaf motif. From Farmana-1.

10 Sherd of a red ware, with incised zigzag lines. From Girawad-2.

11 Sherd of a buff ware painted in black with band and wavy lines. From Farmana-1.

12 Sherd of dull red ware, painted in black. From Kheri Meham.

13 Sherd of dull red ware, painted in black with band. From Kheri Meham.

HARAPPAN POTTERY

The third group of ceramic industry in our region is the Harappan pottery. The Harappan pottery has generally a red surface and is wheel-made, although handmade specimens are also available. The clay is well levitated. The regular striation marks suggest the use of fast spinning wheel.

The Harappan pottery is characterized by its typical painted designs. Paintings in black pigment are invariable arranged in horizontal registers on a carefully-prepared red ground. The designs are horizontal hands, dots, arch, linear and geometrical patterns within the bands of a deeply undulating band, diamond or chess-board pattern, dividing the panel into a number of compartments in which human figures, birds, fish, animals and trees are depicted. Fish-scales, loops, chain patterns, intersecting circles and plant motifs, such as acacia and pipal leaf, are other motifs.

The main shapes are dish-on-stand, beaker, goblet, basin, bowl, cylindrical jar, handled cup, perforated jar, storage jar, 'S'-shaped jar, etc. All these shapes were collected from the area under present study. The remains of the Harappan times were recovered from Farmana-1, Farmana-3, Bhaini Surjan-3, Girawad-2, Kheri Meham, Seman-1 and Seman-6.

DESCRIPTION OF ILLUSTRATED SPECIMENS

Figure 33

1 Fragment of a basin-cum-bowl with a beaded rim and tapering sides. It is of medium to coarse fabric burnt to brick red core. From Farmana-1.

2 Fragment of a basin-cum-bowl having a thickened rim with a depression on the external side to receive a lid. Decorated with incised horizontal lines. Painted with black band on the rim over light red slip. From Farmana-1.

3 Fragment of a basin-cum-bowl having a thickened rim with a depression on the external side to receive a lid and tapering sides. Decorated with incised horizontal lines and concentric circles. Painted in black band on the rim. From Farmana-1.

4 Bowl with a beaded rim and a carinated shoulder. It is of medium fabric, light red core and dull slip. From Farmana-1.

5 Fragment of a bowl, having a thickened rim with a depression on the internal side to receive a lid. Painted in black with horizontal lines on the shoulder and the lower body. From Farmana-1.

6 Bowl with an out-curved rim, convex sides and a rounded bottom. Painted with black horizontal lines at the shoulder. From Farmana-1.

7 Fragment of bowl, with an out-curved rim. It is of medium to coarse fabric, burnt to brick red core. It is painted with black bands at the bally. It bears three Harappan letters. From Farmana-1.

8 Fragment of a dish, with a collared rim. From Farmana-1.

9 Dish-on-stand with a low pedestal, of medium fabric. From Farmana-1.

10 Fragment of a base of a jar. It is of fine fabric and treated with fine red slip over a pale red surface. From Farmana-1.

11 Stem of a dish-on-stand of fine fabric and red in colour. From Farmana-1.

12 Sherd of study red ware vertically incised. It is of medium fabric. From Farmana-1.

13 Sherd of a red ware, painted in black over a red slip. It is of fine fabric. From Farmana-1.

14 Fragment of a perforated jar of red ware. From Farmana-1.

15 Sherd of a buff ware, painted in black. From Farmana-1.

16 Sherd of a red ware, decorated with incised circles. From Farmana-1.

Figure 34

1 Fragment of perforated jar of red ware with an out-turned rim. From Girawad-2.

2 Fragment of perforated jar of red ware. From Kheri Meham.

3 Fragment of perforated jar of red ware. From Farmana-3.

4 Fragment of a lid, with a knob. From Farmana-1.

5 Sherd of red ware, decorated with a nail pattern, incised lines and a black band around them. From Farmana -1.

6 Sherd of red slipped ware, painted in black with triangles and a pipal leaf. It is of thick section and of very fine fabric. From Farmana-1.

7 Sherd of red ware, decorated with nail pattern. From Farmana-1.

8 Sherd of red ware, decorated in black with bands and peacock. From Farmana-1.

9 Sherd of red ware of thick section and fine fabric. Painted in black with opposite triangles above a leaf motif. From Farmana-1.

10 Sherd of red ware of thick section and fine fabric. Painted in black with pipal leaf motif. From Kheri Meham.

11 Sherd of red ware, painted in black colour over a fine red slip. From Farmana-1.

12 Sherd of red ware, decorated with a fish scale pattern. It is of fine fabric, burnt to brick red core and devoid of any surface treatment. From Girawad-2.

Figure 35

A basin with an out-curved rim. It is of medium fabric, burnt to brick red core. From Kheri Meham.

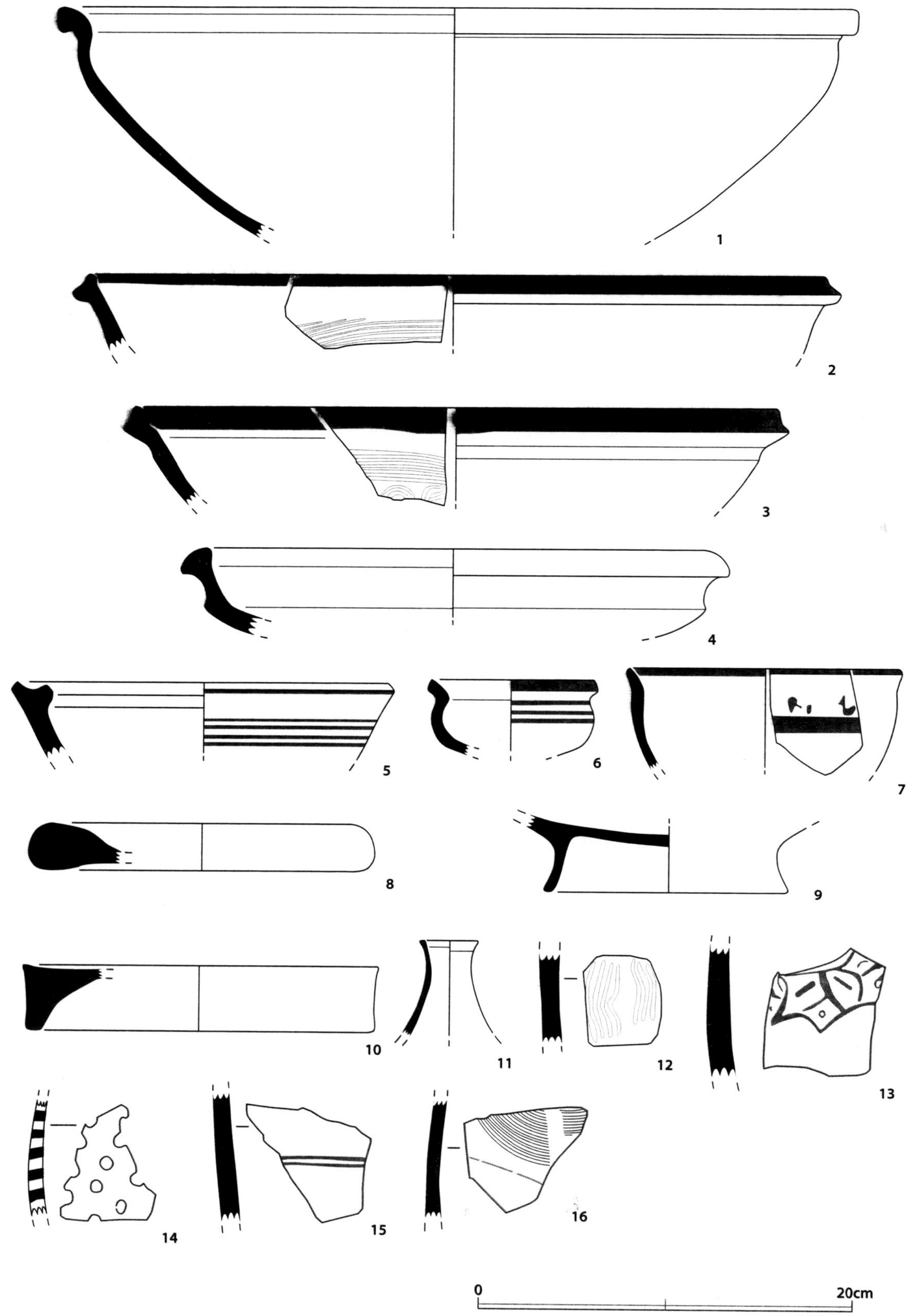

Figure 33 Mature Harappan pottery from Farmana-1 (1:3)

Figure 34 Mature Harappan pottery from the Meham Block

Figure 35 Mature Harappan Pottery from Kheri Meham

LATE HARAPPAN POTTERY

The fourth group of the ceramic industry in the region is the Late Harappan pottery and 30 sites have been found in the region under study, which yielded this group of pottery.

The term 'Late Harappan period' in contra-distinction to the early and middle stages of development of the Harappan culture, implies a stage of decline and decay from the viewpoint of the cyclic concept of cultural development. The pottery of the Late Harappan period is of medium fabric, slightly inferior in levigation to that of the classical Harappan period. It is predominantly wheel-thrown and a tendency towards thicker and sturdier vessels can be clearly discerned. It is treated with light or dull red slip, the bright slip of the classical Harappan being absent. The following is the diagnostic types, all derived from the Harappan shapes.

1) Storage jar with a wide mouth and a thick projected rim.
2) Storage jar with a narrow mouth, a thick projected rim and a tapering shoulder.
3) Storage jar with a narrow mouth, a beaded or collared rim and a globular body.
4) Vase with a beaded or beaked rim, a high concave neck, a globular body and a disc base.
5) Tall vase with a flaring rim and a constricted foot.
6) Dish-on-stand with a projected rim, a carinated shoulder and a tall stand flanged at the top.
7) Dish-on-stand with a drooping rim and a broad squat stand.
8) Dish-on-stand with a deep dish, a projected undercut rim and a squat stand.

Certain classical Harappan shapes such as beakers, goblet, perforated jar and 'S'-shaped jar fall out of use. The typical shapes of the pottery are the following.

1) Jar with a fluted rim, a high neck and a globular body.
2) Vase with a fluted rim, a high neck and a globular body.
3) Vase with an obliquely cut and out-turned rim and a globular body.
4) *Lota*-shaped vase.
5) Vase with a loop handle.
6) Bowl with convex sides.
7) Bowl with a reverted rim and a carinated shoulder.
8) Bowl with a flaring rim and a ring base.
9) Basin with a flaring rim.
10) Basin with an undercut rim and a pedestal base.
11) Trough with shallow grooves on the interior.
12) Bowl-cum-lid.

The Late Harappan pottery is in general profusely painted and decorated with incised designs. The paintings are generally executed in black over a red slip. At times, chocolate pigment is used over a pinkish red or buffish background. The use of red colour in addition to black is sometimes noticed on the Late Harappan pottery of Gujarat. The main designs comprise linear, geometric and naturalistic motifs. The naturalistic designs are generally stylized. The common linear designs include black bands, horizontal, vertical, oblique, zigzag lines and loops. The geometric designs comprise hatched triangles, diamonds and rectangles, semicircles, criss-crosses, chevrons, opposed triangles, ladders and Maltese cross. Among the naturalistic motifs may be mentioned branches, hatched leaves, flowers, lotuses with stalks, honeycombs, eyelid designs, horns, fish, peacock, cranes, etc. The reserved slip technique is found on a few sherds from Mitathal Period IIB in a crude way.

DESCRIPTION OF ILLUSTRATED SPECIMENS

Figure 36

1 Dish-on-stand with a thick and slightly drooping

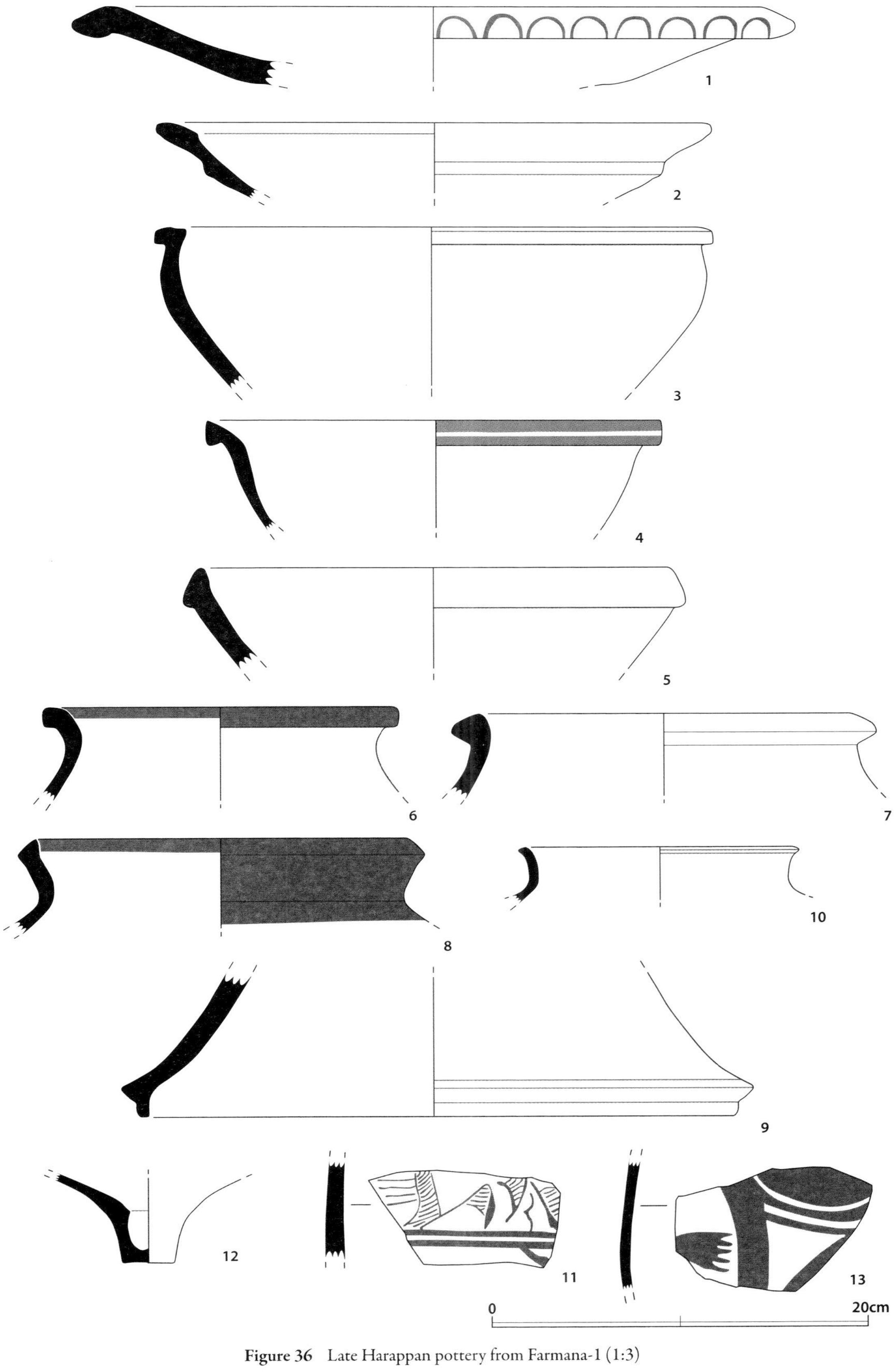

Figure 36 Late Harappan pottery from Farmana-1 (1:3)

clubbed rim. Painted with loop motifs at rim. Medium fabric, pinkish red core and plum red slip. From Farmana-1.

2 Dish with a projected rim and a carinated shoulder. Pinkish red core and matt red surface. From Farmana-1.

3 Fragment of a basin, with a beaded rim and tapering sides. Greyish core, pale or pinkish matt red slip. From Farmana-1.

4 Fragment of a bowl, with a flaring undercut rim and tapering sides. Painted with black band at rim. Medium fabric and light red core. From Farmana-1.

5 Fragment of a bowl, with a beaded rim and tapering sides. Medium fabric and pinkish red core, pale pinkish matt red slip. From Farmana-1.

6 Fragment of a vase, with a flaring rim. Medium fabric and light red core. From Farmana-1.

7 Fragment of a jar, with a beaded rim and medium fabric. From Farmana-1.

8 Fragment of a jar of medium thickness, with an everted rim. Painted in black with horizontal bands above shoulder. From Farmana-1.

9 Stem of a dish-on-stand with a flanged base. From Farmana-1.

10 Vase with a short everted rim. Medium fabric, dull red core and dull red slip. From Farmana-1.

11 Sherd of a medium thick red ware. Painted with black horizontal bands with rosette motifs. From Farmana-1.

12 Fragment of a lid-cum-bowl of dull red ware. From Farmana-1.

13 Sherd of a medium thin red ware. Painted with black band and sun motifs. From Farmana-1.

Figure 37

1 A collarless pot with an oval shape and a disc base. Medium fabric. Painted with birds and other floral design. This burial urn was found from Bedwa-2.

2 Dish-on-stand with a projected rim, a carinated shoulder and a stand with everted base. Ribbed below the juncture between the dish and the stand.Pinkish red core. From Bedwa-2.

3 Bowl-on-stand with a flaring and projected rim, ribbed below the juncture between the bowl and the stand. Pinkish red core. From Bedwa-2.

Figure 38

1 Vase with a beaded rim, a globular body and a disc base. Medium fabric. Painted with black horizontal bands at rim, shoulder and belly, and wavy lines at shoulder. From Bedwa-2.

2 A Vase with an out-turned beaded rim and a globular body. Painted with black band above shoulder and two horizontal bands near belly. It is of medium fabric, light red core and light slip applied on surface. From Bedwa-2.

Figure 39

1 A base of goblet with a footed base. Medium fabric, red core. From Bedwa-2.

2 Vase with a splayed-out rim and disc base. Medium fabric light red core. From Bedwa-2.

Figure 40

A jar with a beaded rim, a high neck and an ovoid body. Painted with horizontal bands at rim, neck, shoulder and belly. Rusticated on the lower part of the body. From Bedwa-2.

Figure 41

Fragment of a storage jar, with a beaked rim and a globular body. Painted in black with horizontal lines with loops near neck and two horizontal black bands near shoulder. Medium fabric and pinkish red core. From Kheri Meham.

PAINTED GREY WARE AND ASSOCIATED WARES

The Painted Grey Ware or PGW, with uniform grey surface and painted designs in black, has been regarded as the hallmark of the culture to which

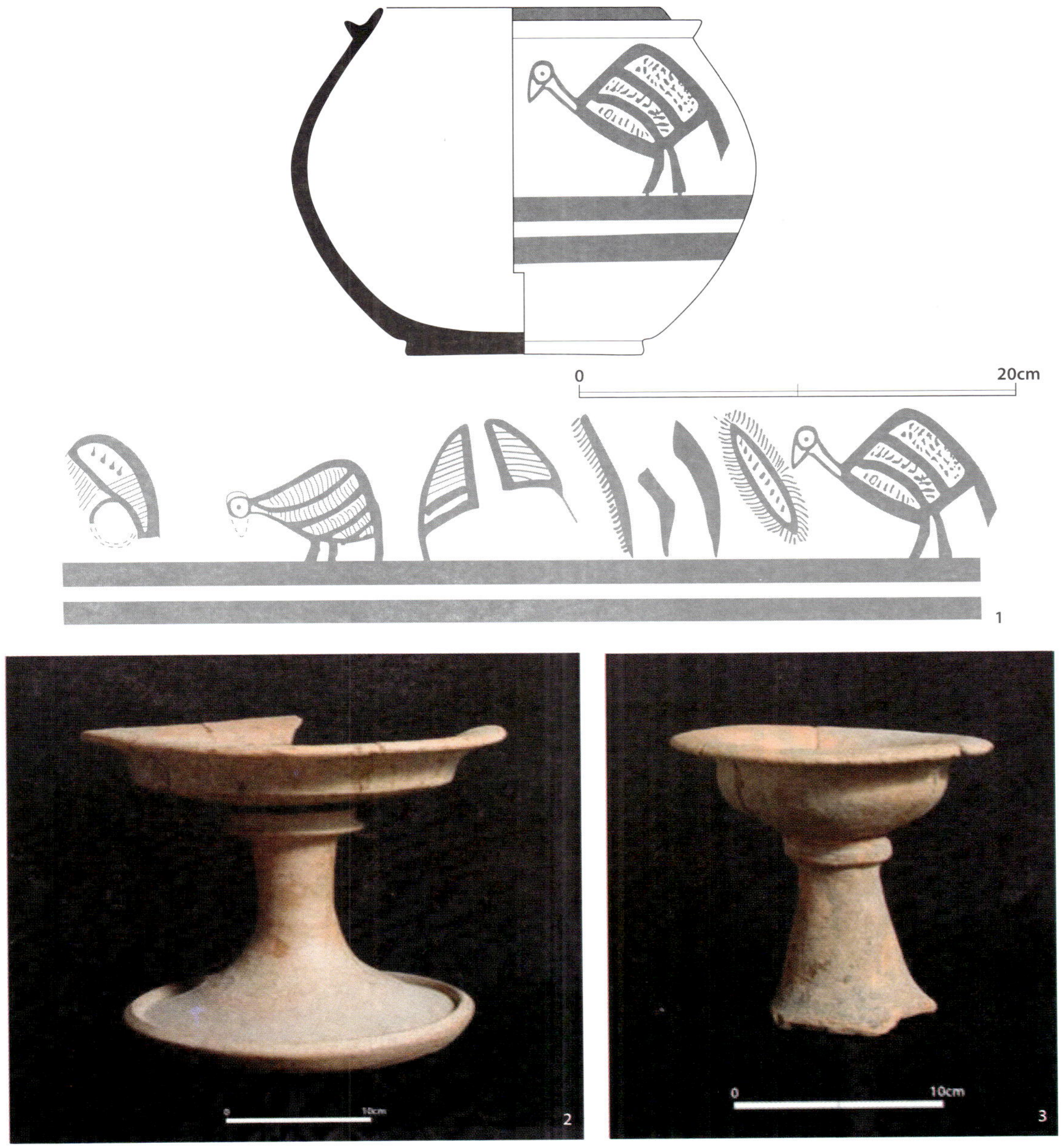

Figure 37 Mature or Late Harappan Pottery from Bedwa-2

it belongs and which has been named after it. Its distribution is confined to a specific geographical horizon, i.e. Punjab, Haryana and the upper Ganga Valley.

The common shapes are bowl and dish. The main types of the bowl are those with straight tapering convex or concave sides or corrugated one. The dish type has more restricted variety generally with a vertical or inturned featureless rim, a rounded, straight or tapering sides, a convex body and a carination near the sagger base. They are fairly large with a diameter of above 20 cm. It has been suggested that they were used for dining purpose.

The decorative paintings occurring on both the inner and outer surface are in black or in deep chocolate, executed before firing. The designs consist of simple geometric patterns like bands and strokes of vertical and standing lines, dots and dashes, chains,

Figure 38 Late Harappan Pottery from Bedwa-2

Figure 39 Late Harappan Pottery from Bedwa-2

Figure 40 Late Harappan Pottery from Bedwa-2

loops, etc.

The PGW is made of well-levigated clay, wheel-thrown, smooth and uniformly blackish grey and ash grey in colour, representing a highly-developed technique in ceramic manufacture and an especially elegant achievement of the Indian potter of those times.

In association with PGW, red ware is also found. The red ware is made of carelessly levitated clay usually mixed with small *kankers* and husk. The shapes of this ware include basin, bowl, vase, jar, etc. This was the common ware of the PGW assemblage.

Figure 42

1 Dish of PGW with a sharply-inturned featureless rim and sides carinated to a sagger base. It is painted in black on the exterior with groups of oblique strokes below the rim and a horizontal black band around rim. From Madina-2.

2 Fragment of PGW with a sharply inturned featureless rim and sides carinated to a sagger base. It is painted on the exterior in black with some oblique strokes and a horizontal hand around rim. From Ganganagar-1.

3 Fragment of a dish of black slipped ware, with a vertical featureless rim and sides sharply carinated towards the base. Medium fabric. From Mokhra-5.

4 Fragment of a bowl of grey ware, with a vertical featureless rim and sides sharply carinated towards the base. Very fine fabric. From Nindana-7.

5 Dish of PGW, with an internally shortened rim and incurved sides. It is painted in black on the interior with groups of wavy lines and on the exterior with a group of oblique strokes thinning towards the lower end. From Bedwa-4.

6 Fragment of a dish of grey ware with a slightly incurved featureless rim. Medium fabric. From Ajaib-1.

7 Fragment of a dish of PGW, with a slightly incurved featureless rim. Fine fabric. Painted in black

Figure 41 Late Harappan Pottery from Kheri Meham

with a band at the rim From Bharan-1.

8 Fragment of a vase of red ware with an everted, externally oval rim. It is devoid of any slip or wash. From Madina-2.

9 Fragment of a vase of red ware with a vertically- and externally-clubbed rim and a bluntly carinated neck. It is devoid of slip or wash. From Bedwa-3.

10 Fragment of a miniature pot of red ware, with a horizontally-splayed-out rim and a concave neck. From Girawad-1.

Figure 43

1 A vase of red ware, with a slightly out-turned rim, a high neck and a rounded body. From Madina-2.

2 Fragment of a bowl of grey ware, turned to red due to over heating. Painted in black on the external side with a horizontal band on the rim, two vertical and a oblique lines with a design of concentric semicircles. From Madina-2.

Figure 44

1 Fragment of a deep bowl of Black Slipped Ware. From Madina-2.

2 Fragment of dish of grey ware, with an inturned featureless rim. Painted in black on the interior with a black horizontal band on the rim above two groups of oblique lines. From Madina-2.

3 Fragment of disc of grey ware, with an inturned featureless rim and flat base. From Madina-2.

Figure 45

1 Fragment of a bowl of grey ware, with a vertical and internally-sharpened rim and rounded sides. It is painted in black on the interior with a horizontal band on the rim above two groups of oblique lines with concentric circles. From Bedwa-3.

2 Fragment of bowl of grey ware, painted in black on interior with two group of concentric semicircles, placed opposite to each. From Madina-2.

3 Fragment of PGW, painted in black on the

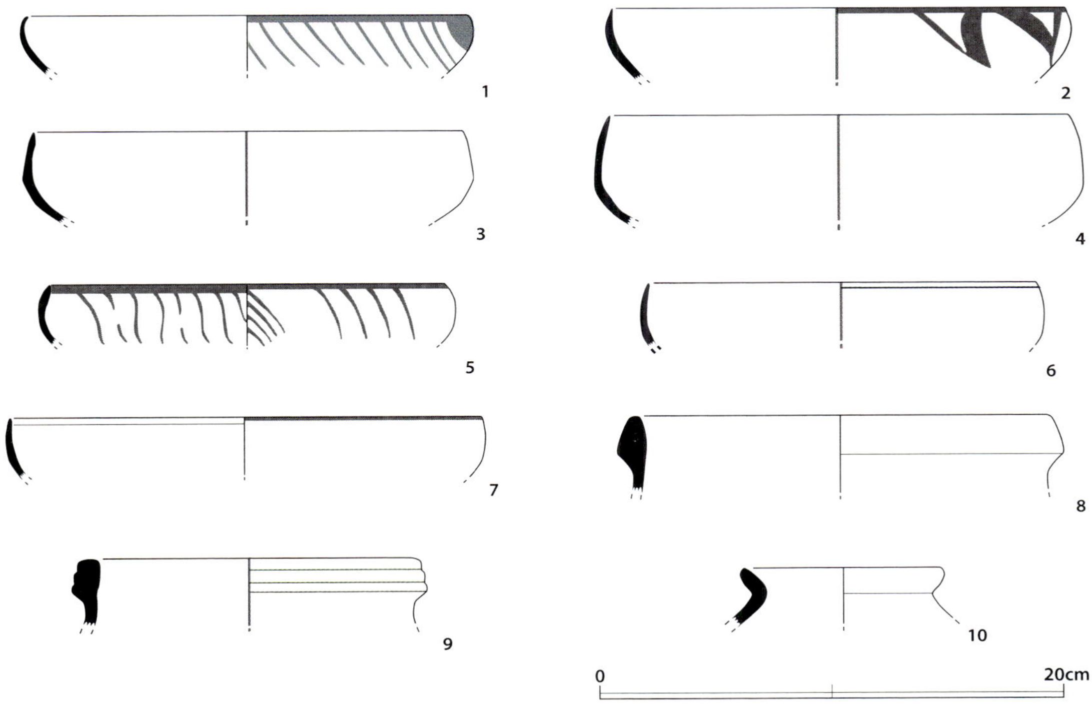

Figure 42 PGW from the Meham Block (1:3)

Figure 43 PGW from Madina-2

Figure 44 PGW from Madina-2

Figure 45 PGW from the Meham Block

Figure 46 Black Slipped Ware from Madina-2

Figure 47 PGW from Madina-2

exterior with a black horizontal band, from Bahelba-3.

4 Fragment of bowl of PGW, with a vertically-sharpened rim and slightly tapering sides. It is painted in black on the exterior with a horizontal band on the rim above intersecting loops. From Bhaini Bharo-2.

5 Fragment of a base of PGW, painted in black on interior with two groups of oblique lines. From Madina-2.

6 Fragment of a base of PGW, painted in black on interior with a design framed by two intersecting rows of three lines. From Bharan-2.

7 Fragment of a base of PGW, painted in black on the interior with one concentric circle enclosed by dots on three sides. From Girawad-1.

8 Fragment of grey ware, decorated with stamped circles. From Madina-2.

9 Fragment of a bowl of PGW, painted with black on interior with wavy lines. From Madina-2.

10 Fragment of PGW, painted in black on interior with concentric circle. From Madina-2.

11 Fragment of PGW, painted in black on exterior with a horizontal band on the rim above oblique strokes on the body. From Kharkhra-1.

12 Fragment of PGW, painted in black on the interior with oblique strokes. From Kharkhra-1.

13 Fragment of a base of PGW, painted in black on the interior with intersecting strokes. From Madina-3.

14 Fragment of PGW, painted in black on the interior with concentric semicircles. From Meham -4.

15 Fragment of PGW, painted in black on the interior with two groups of dashes. From Mokhra-2.

16 Fragment of a bowl of PGW, painted in black on the interior with a horizontal band on the rim above four vertical lines on the body. From Mokhra-5.

17 Fragment of PGW, painted in black on the interior with irregular semicircles. From Nindana-2.

18 Fragment of PGW, painted in black on the exterior with three oblique lines. From Nindana-7.

19 Hopscotch made of a PGW sherd, painted in black on the exterior with two groups of concentric semicircles. From Madina-2.

20 Fragment of PGW, painted in black on the interior with a horizontal band on the rim above intersecting zigzag lines on the body. From Seman-5.

Figure 46

1-3 Dish of black slipped ware, with a vertical featureless rim, straight sides and a flat base. Fine fabric. From Madina-2.

Figure 47

1-2 Deep bowls of grey ware, with a vertically- and internally-sharpened rim, straight sides and a flat base. Both specimens are painted in black on the exterior with a horizontal band on the rim. From Madina-2.

EARLY HISTORICAL AND HISTORICAL POTTERY

The sixth group of ceramic industry in the Meham Block is the Early Historical and Historical red ware. This type of pottery is made on a wheel and has coarse fabric. Most of the pots are treated with light red wash or slip. The main shapes in this group include storage jar, vase, basin, incurved bowl, lid, etc.

Figure 48

1 Fragment of a vase with an out-turned and rounded collared rim with a groove on the external side. Dull red surface and medium fabric. From Bedwa-1.

2 Fragment of a vase of red ware, with an out-turned rim with a groove on the external side. Medium fabric and treated with a red wash. From Bedwa-3.

3 Fragment of a vase of dull red ware, with a vertically- and externally-collared rim and corrugated shoulder. From Meham-1.

4 Fragment of a vase of red ware, with an out-curved featureless rim. More prominently ridged above the neck. Medium fabric. From Behelba-4.

5 Bowl of dull red ware, with an obliquely-sharpened rim and sides tapering to a flat and thickened base. Medium fabric, devoid of any wash. From Madina-2.

6 Lid of dull red ware with a featureless rim. It is sharply carinated to a flat base. Medium fabric. From Farmana-3.

7 Lid of dull red ware with an externally- and vertically-cut and flaring rim, a solid central knob on the interior and a flattish thickened base. Coarse fabric, devoid of any slip or wash. From Farmana-1.

8 Fragment of a vase of red ware with an out-turned thickened rim and a concave neck. Comparatively fine fabric. From Bhaini Surjan-1.

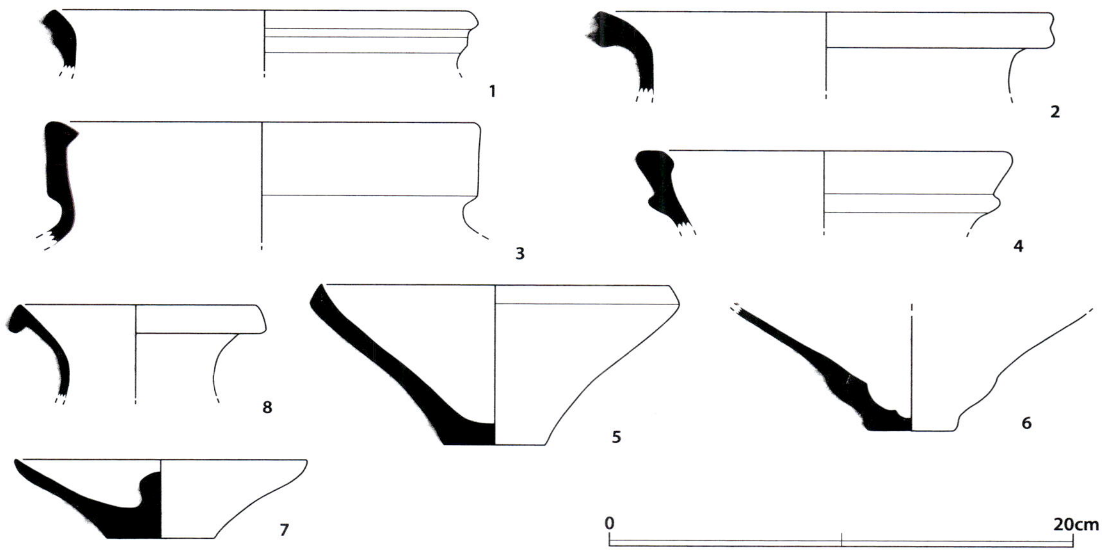

Figure 48 Early Historical and Historical pottery from the Meham Block (1:3)

Figure 49 Historical pottery from Madina-IV

Figure 49
1-2 Incurved rim bowls with a flat base, burnt to brick red colour. From Madina-4.

Figure 50
1-3 Knife-edged-rim bowls with a flat base. From Behelba-3.

MEDIEVAL POTTERY

The eighth and last group of ceramic industry in the region under present study in the Early Medieval and Medieval pottery. This type of ceramic were found at 37 sites in this region. The pottery consist totally of red ware. Pots are wheel-made and generally have a medium to coarse fabric. It is painted with liner patterns, decorated with notches arranged horizontally. The main shapes in this pottery are knife-edged-rim bowl, basin, dish, *handi*, jar, lid and vase, etc.

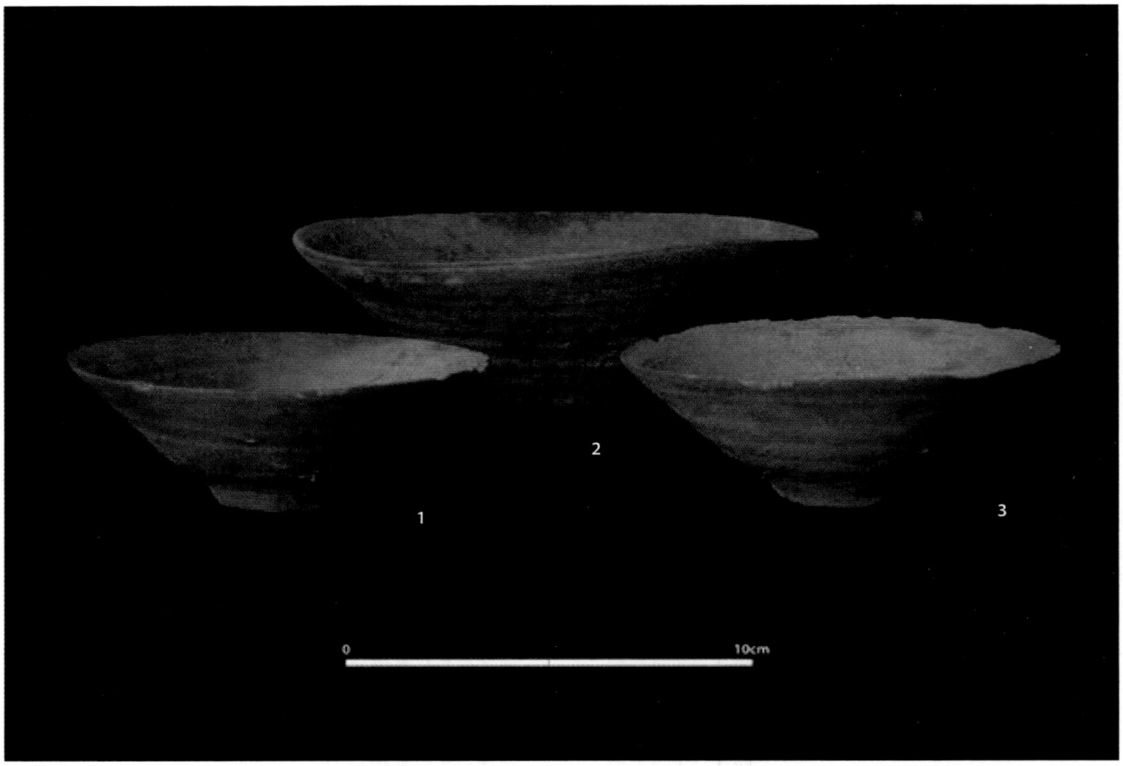

Figure 50 Historical pottery from the Meham Block

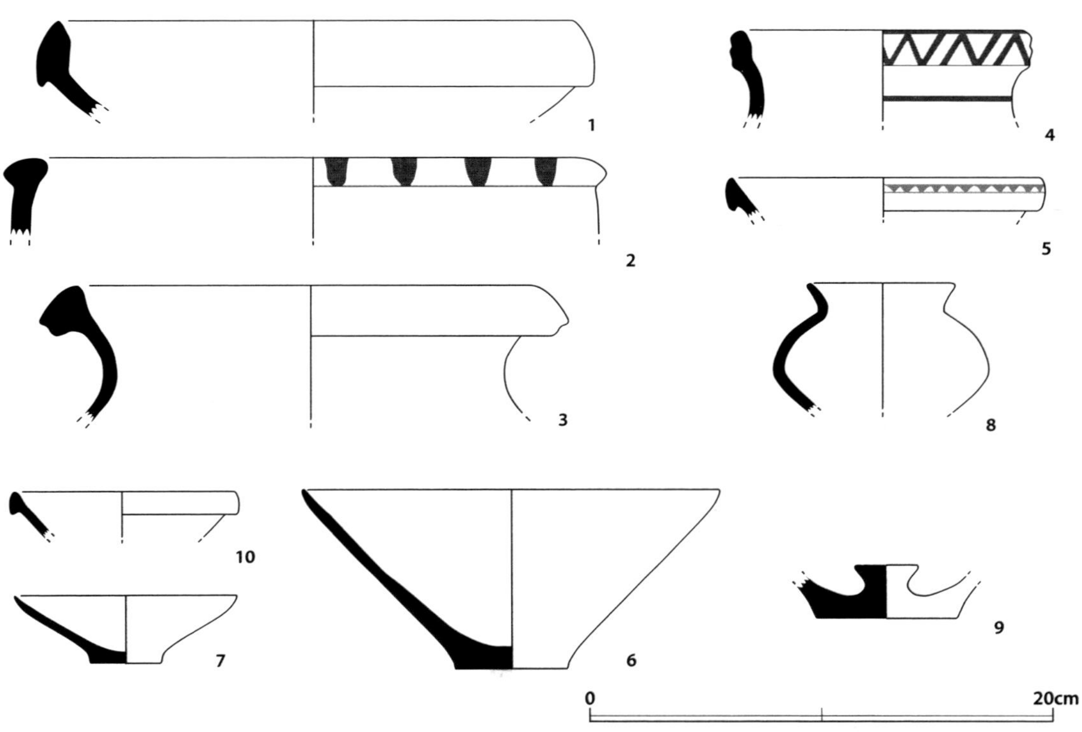

Figure 51 Early Medieval and Medieval pottery from the Meham Block (1:3)

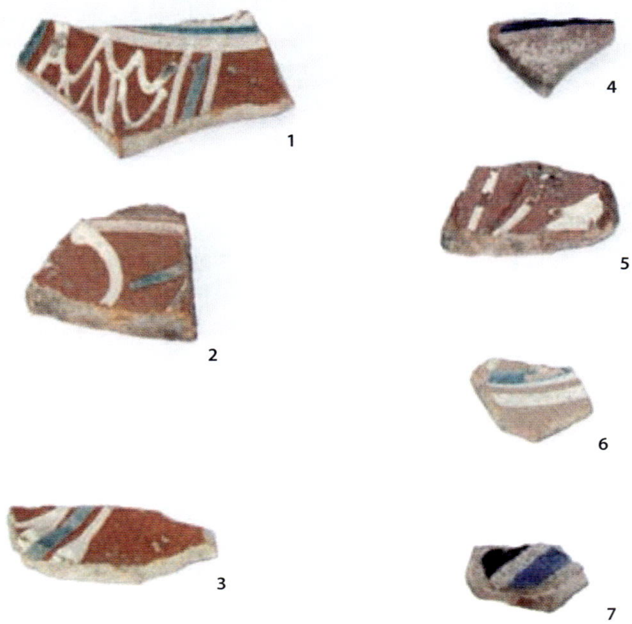

Figure 52 Medieval Pottery from Meham-2

DESCRIPTION OF ILLUSTRATED SPECIMENS

Figure 51

1 Fragment of a basin with a collared rim. Medium fabric red ware. From Meham-1.

2 Fragment of a basin of medium fabric red ware. From Behelba-2.

3 Fragment of a vase of red ware, with an out-turned and grooved rim and a concave neck. Coarse fabric and dull red surface. From Bhaini Surjan-1.

4 Fragment of a vase of red ware, with an out-turned rim with grooves and a small vertical stroke on the exterior. The rim is pained in black with zigzig lines. From Meham-2.

5 Fragment of a vase of red ware. The rim is painted in black. From Ajaib-1.

6 Bowl of dull red ware with a sharpened-knife-edged rim, a carinated body and a flat base. Medium fabric, devoid of any slip or wash. From Kheri Meham.

7 Small bowl of dull red ware, sharpened-knife-edged rim and a flat base. Medium fabric, devoid of any slip. From Kheri Meham.

8 Fragment of a vase, with an out-turned featureless rim. Medium fabric. From Bedwa-1.

9 Small lid of dull red ware with a flaring rim, a solid central knob on the interior and a flattish thick base. Medium fabric. From Farmana-2.

10 Fragment of a bowl of dull red ware. From Farmana-1.

Figure 52

1-7 Fragments of Islamic glazed ware. From Meham-2.

CHAPTER V

STUDY OF MISCELLANEOUS OBJECTS

Different material remains of ancient cultures, such as ornaments, toys, household utensils, human and animal figures, etc., were found during the course of exploration. These remains are the important tools for the reconstruction of various aspects of ancient cultures and their socio-economic life. They are not only the art pieces but represent the activities of people in an unknown society for which we have no other documentary evidences. It will have to be admitted that thousands of pages or words may be unable to convey the inner feeling and ideas of people in the manner in which they are revealed by the finds associated with the ancient culture.

During the exploration in Meham Block of Rohtak District, the researcher has brought to light a variety of miscellaneous finds of stone, terracotta, shell, glass, carnelian, agate, lapis lazuli, gold, steatite, copper, etc., from his discovered archaeological sites ranging from pre-Harappan to Medieval times in the region of present study. Of these, 265 antiquities have been selected to be illustrated in this work. These miscellaneous antiquities are beads, bangles, sling balls, cakes, '8'-shaped cakes (*mustika*), animal and human figures, wheel, copper spearhead, and arrowhead, etc. The chronological position of these finds could be possible by typological comparison and on the basis of culture of their findspot. The description of these antiquities is given below material-wise.

TERRACOTTA CAKES

Terracotta cakes are the important finds from the region under the present study. These terracotta cakes are both triangular and round *mustika*. All these types of terracotta cakes are found from different Harappan sites. During the Harappan times triangular and *mustika*-type cakes were used, while during the Late Harappan times cakes of circular shape as well as both these types were used. What may have been the use of these cakes, which are found in a great number at all the Harappan sites, is shrouded in mystery. Some scholars are of the opinion that these were used for religious purpose. This view seems to carry some weight because even in present day terracotta cakes or cakes of cow dung are used for worshipping purpose.

DESCRIPTION OF ILLUSTRATED SPECIMENS

Figure 53

1 Triangular cake of the Harappan period. From Farmana-1.

2 Triangular cake of the Harappan period. From Farmana-1.

3 Triangular cake of the Harappan period. From Kheri-Meham.

4 Triangular cake of the Harappan period. From Farmana-3.

5 *Idli*-shaped cake of the Harappan period. From Kheri Meham.

6 Circular cake of the Early Harappan period. From Girawad-2.

7 Circular cake of the Early Harappan period. From Farmana-1.

8 Circular cake of the Early Harappan period. From Bahelba-2.

9 *Idli*-shaped cake of the Harappan period. From Girawad-3.

10 Circular cake of the Early Harappan period. From Farmana-1.

11 '8'-shaped cake of the Harappan period. From

Figure 53 Terracotta Cakes from the Meham Block

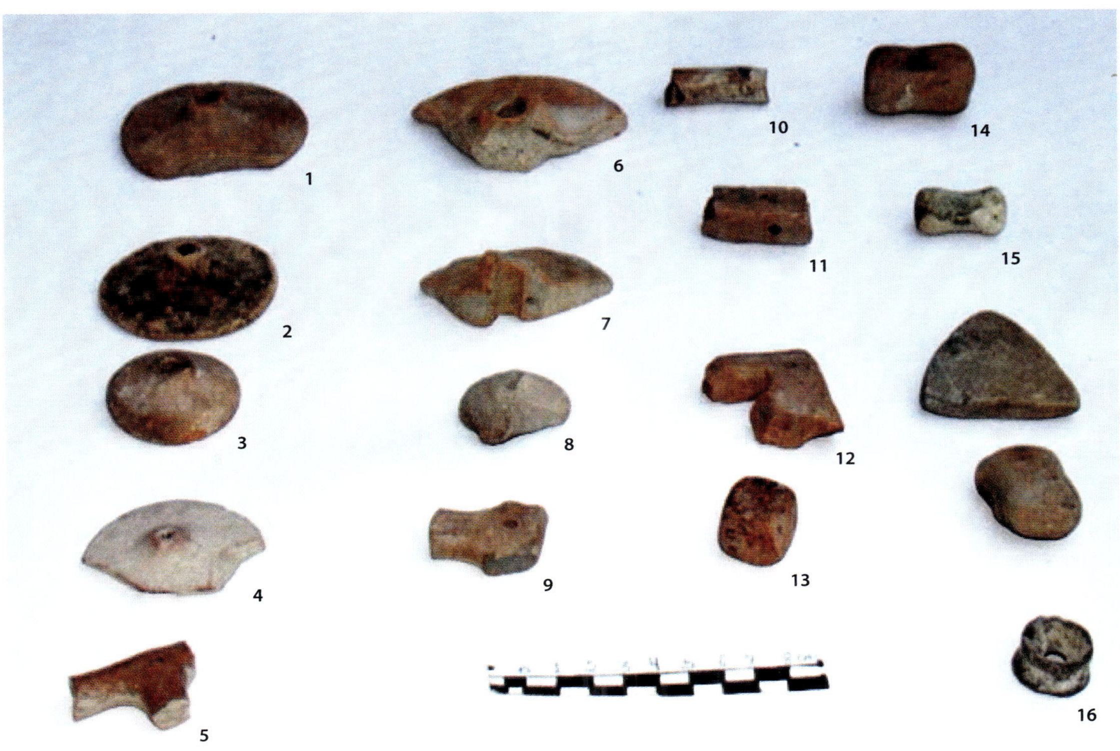

Figure 54 Terracotta wheels, toy cart frames and ear-stud from the Meham Block

Farmana-1.

12 '8'-shaped cake of the Harappan period. From Kheri-Meham.

13 '8'-shaped cake of Early Harappan period. From Seman-1.

14 '8'-shaped cake of the Harappan period. From Farmana-1.

TOY CART FRAME

A few fragmentary toy cart frames were found during the explorations. They are made of terracotta. These carts have the frame whose floor is solid and has holes in it for fixing the axes and wheels.

TOY CART WHEELS

Toy cart wheels are made of terracotta in the same manner as beads and pottery. Sometimes, toy cart wheels have a hub also and these are single-hubbed or double-hubbed ones. The double-hubbed wheels was reversible in fitting and the boss allowed more free play to wheel than it rubbed against the sides of the vehicle. Descriptions of a few specimens discovered from the area are given below.

Figure 54

1 Toy-cart wheel of red ware of the Harappan period. Its inner side is plain, while the outer side is slightly convex and has a protruding hub. From Farmana-1.

2 Toy-cart wheel of red ware of the Harappan period. Its inner side is plain, while the outer side is slightly convex and has a protruding hub. From Kheri Meham.

3 Toy-cart hubbed wheel of the Late Harappan period. From Madina-2.

4 Partially broken toy cart wheel of the Early Harappan period, with a hub on the exterior. From Girawad-2.

5 Fragment of a toy cart frame of the Early Harappan period, with two crossing holes in front and one hole in other side. From Girawad-2.

6 Fragment of a wheel of the Late Harappan period, with a hub on the exterior. From Bahelba-6.

7 Partially broken toy-cart hubbed wheel of the Early Harappan period. From Seman-1.

8 Fragment of a wheel of the Late Harappan period, with a hub on the exterior. From Madina-2.

9 Fragment of a toy cart frame of the Harappan period, with two crossing holes. From Girawad-2.

10 Fragment of a toy cart frame of the Harappan period, having two crossing holes in front and one hole on other side. From Seman-1.

11 Fragment of a toy cart frame of the Harappan period. From Farmana-1.

12 Fragment of a toy cart frame of the Early Harappan period, with two crossing holes in front and one hole on the other side. From Girawad-2.

13 A gamesman of the Harappan period. Square in shape having point from one to six on each side. From Farmana-1.

14 An ear-stud of the Harappan period, from Farmana-1.

15 An ear-stud of the Harappan period, from Farmana-1.

16 A biconical wheel of the Harappan period, grey colour. From Farmana-1.

TERRACOTTA BEADS

A good number of terracotta beads was recovered from various sites belong to different stages of protohistoric, Historical and Medieval times. To have some ideas about the folk art and their uses, some of them are illustrated and described.

DESCRIPTION OF ILLUSTRATED SPECIMENS

Figure 55

1 Terracotta *ghata*-shaped bead of the PGW period, red in colour, truncated apex. From Madina-2.

2 Terracotta *ghata*-shaped bead of the PGW

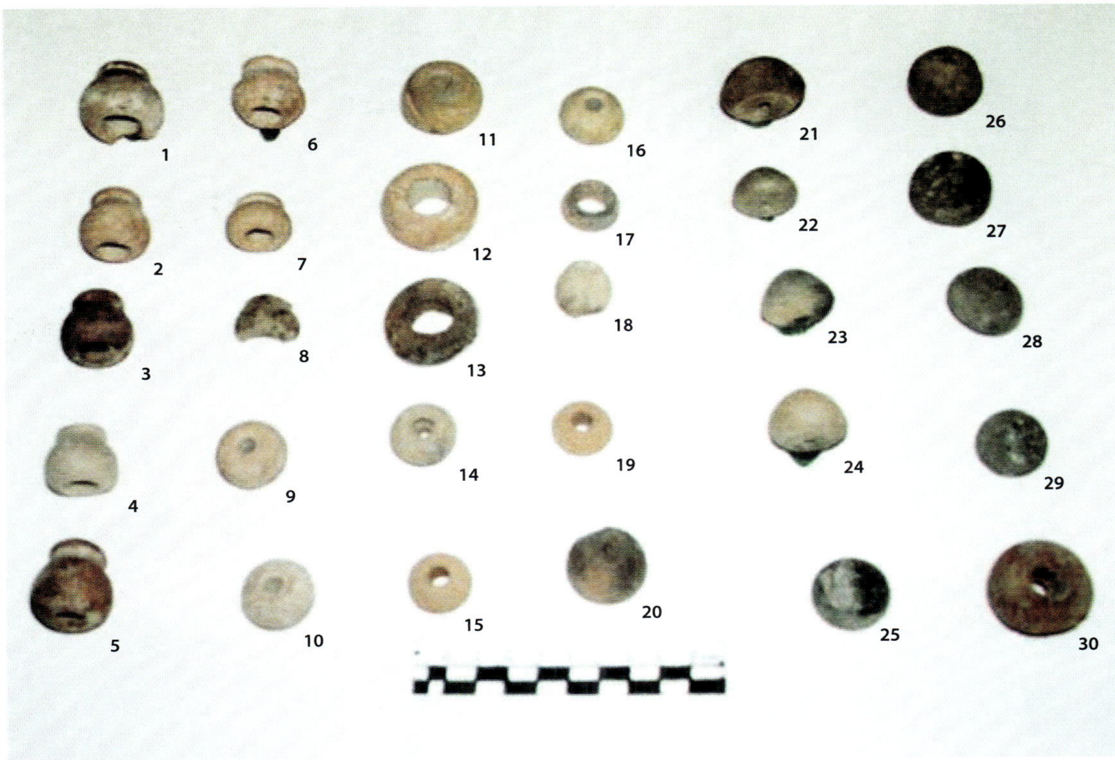

Figure 55 Terracotta beads from the Meham Block

period, red in colour, truncated apex. From Madina-2.

3 Terracotta *ghata*-shaped bead of the PGW period, red in colour, truncated apex. From Madina-2.

4 Terracotta *ghata*-shaped bead of the PGW period, red in colour, truncated apex. From Madina-2.

5 Terracotta *ghata*-shaped bead of the PGW period, red in colour. From Nindana -7.

6 Terracotta *ghata*-shaped bead of the PGW period, red in colour. From Bahelba-2.

7 Terracotta *ghata*-shaped bead of the PGW period. From Mokhra-5.

8 Fragment of *ghata*-shaped bead of PGW period. From Ajaib-1.

9 Small terracotta biconical, circular and truncated bead of the Harappan period. From Farmana-1.

10 Small terracotta biconical, circular and truncated bead of the Harappan period. From Farmana-1.

11 Small terracotta biconical and circular bead of the Harappan period. From Kheri Meham.

12 Small ring-shaped bead of the Harappan period. From Farmana-1.

13 Small ring-shaped bead of the Harappan period. From Farmana-1.

14 Small ring-shaped bead of the Harappan period. From Girawad-2.

15 Small biconical bead of the Harappan period. From Girawad-2.

16 Biconical and truncated bead of the Late Harappan period. From Kheri Meham.

17 Small ring-shaped bead of the Harappan period. From Seman-1.

18 Small terracotta biconical bead of the Late Harappan period. From Madina-2.

19 Terracotta biconical bead of the Late Harappan period. From Madina-2.

20 Terracotta arecanut-shaped bead of the Historical period, having a depression on the top. From Bahelba-2.

21 Terracotta arecanut-shaped beads of the Historical period, having a depression on the top.

Figure 56 Terracotta discs and skin rubbers from the Meham Block

From Bahelba-2.

22 Terracotta arecanut-shaped bead of the Historical period, having a depression on the top. From Bahelba-2.

23 Terracotta arecanut-shaped bead of the Historical period, having a depression on the top. From Bahelba-2.

24 Terracotta arecanut-shaped bead of the Historical period. From Madina-2.

25 Terracotta arecanut-shaped bead of the Historical period. From Madina-2.

26 Terracotta arecanut-shaped bead of the Historical period. From Madina-2.

27 Terracotta arecanut-shaped bead of the Historical period. From Madina-2.

28 Terracotta arecanut-shaped bead of the Historical period. From Kheri Meham.

29 Terracotta arecanut-shaped bead of the Historical period. From Farmana-2.

30 Terracotta circular bead of the Harappan period. From Seman-1.

Figure 56

1 Terracotta disc, partlaly broken. Decorated by notches or nail impressions around the circumference on both sides. Grey in colour. Datable to the PGW period. From Madina-2.

2 Terracotta disc of the PGW period decorated with nail impressions around the circumference on both sides. Red in colour and treated with a lustrous slip. From Madina-2.

3 Terracotta disc of the PGW period, decorated with nail impressions around the circumference on both sides. Red in colour and treated with lustrous slip. From Madina-2.

4 Terracotta disc of the PGW period, decorated with nail impressions around the circumference on both sides. Red in colour and treated with lustrous slip. From Madina-2.

5 Pottery disc of red ware of the PGW period,

circular in shape. From Nindana-7.

6 Pottery disc of the Late Harappan period, made from a Late Harappan red ware sherd, having grounded edges and a circular shape. From Ajaib-2.

7 Terracotta disc of the PGW period, decorated with nail impressions around the circumference on both sides. Red in colour and treated with lustrous slip. From Ajaib-2.

8 Pottery disc of the Late Harappan period, made of a red ware sherd of the Late Harappan pottery, having grounded edges and a circular shape. From Ajaib-2.

9 Pottery disc of the Late Harappan period, made of red ware sherd of the Late Harappan pottery, having grounded edges and a circular shape. From Ajaib-2.

10 Terracotta disc of the PGW period, decorated with notches around the circumference on both sides. Grey in colour. From Ajaib-2.

11 Pottery disc of the Early Harappan period, having grounded edges and a circular shape from Kheri Meham.

12 Pottery disc of the Early Harappan period, having grounded edges and a circular in shape. From Kheri Meham.

13 Terracotta flesh rubber of the Early Historical period, with small chips of black granite. From Madina-2.

14 Terracotta flesh rubber of the Early Historical period, with small chips of black granite. From Madina-2.

TERRACOTTA ART

Terracotta represents a common folk art depicting the aspiration, inclinations, traditions and religious feelings of people. These terracotta art can be divided in according with their chronology. These may be handmade or prepared from moulds. Actually the terracotta represents a common people's belief, faiths, and pleasure.

Clay has been regarded as the primeval plastic material on account of its easy tractability and easiness to be shaped when wet. A more or less durable form can be produced either by hardening through exposure in sun or firing.

The beginning of plastic practices in India can be traced in the early farming communities of Baluchisthan. Sites in this region have furnished a fairly good number of terracotta animal and women figurines. During the Mature Harappan, Late Harappan and PGW periods, the material for plastic art was mainly terracotta.

Not only during the protohistoric times but also in the Historical and Medieval times, the terracotta seems to have been a favourite medium of representing the plastic art. Almost every site in India has yielded a considerable number of terracotta objects of varied shapes and forms. The area under present study has also yielded some terracotta figurines during exploration, which are described below.

DESCRIPTION OF ILLUSTRATED SPECIMENS

Figure 57

Terracotta figurine representing an elephant. Legs and tail of the figurine are partly broken. It has a pair of lozenge eyes and is decorated with three incised lines and incised dots between lines. It is made of well-levitated clay, well fired and treated with red slip. On the artistic basis, it can be dated to the Mauryan or Sunga periods. From Bahelba-2.

Figure 58

Terracotta figurine representing an elephant. The hind legs are totally broken, while the fronts are partly broken. It is decorated with stamped leaf designs on forehead. It has a pair of lozenge eyes. This figurine is made of well-levigated clay but is ill fired, treated with red slip. On the basis of its stylistic features, it can be dated to the Mauryan or Sunga periods. From Bahelba-2.

Figure 57 Terracotta animal figurine from Bahelba-2

Figure 58 Terracotta animal figurine from Bahelba-2

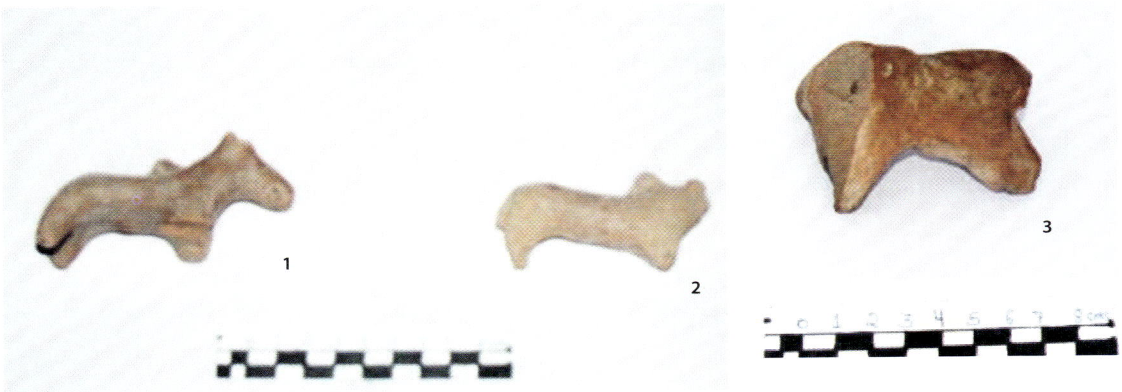

Figure 59 Terracotta animal figurines from Farmana-1 (3-4) and Meham-2 (5)

Figure 60 Teracotta animal figurine from Meham-2

Figure 59

1 Figurine of a humped bull of the Harappan period, having a proportionate appliqué hump. Its legs are broken. There is a horizontal hole near nose for piercing a string. From Farmana-1.

2 Fragment of a broken terracotta bull figurine of the Harappan period, having a proportionate appliqué hump. Legs and neck are broken. From Farmana-1.

3 Terracotta figurine representing a horse. The neck and tail are completely broken, while legs are partly broken. This robust figurine of horse is made of well-levigated clay. But it is slightly ill fired and treated with red slip. Appliqué lines represent the caparisons. This figurine can be associated with the Medieval period. From Meham-2.

Figure 60

The head of an elephant with prominent trunk,

which is slightly broken. Decorated with incised dot design. This crudely finished figurine is made of well-levigated clay and well fired. It can be dated to the Medieval times based on the other cultural materials found from the site together with this figurine. From Meham-2.

STONE TOOLS AND OBJECTS

Several stone, terracotta and faience objects were recovered in the course of exploration. These objects include pestles, sling balls, weights, etc. Most of these are made of sandstone and constitute the household utensils. These objects belong to different cultures and are the best pieces of their type are described below.

DESCRIPTION OF ILLUSTRATED SPECIMENS

Figure 61

1 Weight made of sandstone of the Harappan period. From Farmana-1.

2 Sling ball of sandstone of the Late Harappan period, traces of pecking visible on the surface. From Kheri-Meham.

3 Sling ball of sandstone of the Late Harappan period. Its surface is relatively smooth. From Kheri Meham.

4 Sling ball of sandstone of Late Harappan period. From Kheri Meham.

5 Ball of sandstone of the Late Harappan period. From Madina-2

6 Weight made of sandstone of the Harappan period. From Girawad-2.

7 Fragment of a faience ball of the Late Harappan period, dark green in colour. From Farmana-1.

8 Terracotta sling ball of the Late Harappan period. From Kheri Meham.

9 A stone sling ball of the Late Harappan period. From Kheri Meham.

10 Sling ball of sandstone of the Late Harappan period. From Ajaib-2.

11 Sling ball of sandstone of the Late Harappan period. From Ajaib-2.

12 Large sling ball of terracotta of the Harappan period. Red in colour, slip applied to the surface. From Farmana-1.

Figure 62

1 Fine specimen of rectangular/wedge-shaped pestle of black granite stone of the PGW period. It bears striations due to grinding on both the rounded ends. From Madina-2.

2 Grinding stone of greyish colour of the Early Medieval period, with a flat grinding surface. From Bhaini Matoo.

3 Grinding stone of grayish colour of the Medieval period. From Meham-2.

4 Grinding stone of the Medieval period, with a smooth surface on the upper side. From Nindana-3.

5 Weight of granite of Early Historical period, black in colour. From Bedwa-3.

6 Pestle made of grey sandstone, roughly triangular shape. From Madina-7.

CHERT OBJECTS

The most predominant tool of the Harappan lithic industry is blade. Chert is very common material found from almost every Harappan site. Chert blades are perfectly symmetric in form and very carefully retouched. The main source for chert during the Harappan period is the Rohari Hills, Pakistan. Some chert objects were recovered in the course of explorations, which are described as follow.

DESCRIPTION OF ILLUSTRATED SPECIMENS

Figure 63

1 Fluted chert core of the Harappan period. From Farmana-1.

2 Fluted chert core of the Harappan period. From Farmana-1.

3 Chert blade of the Harappan period. From Farmana-1.

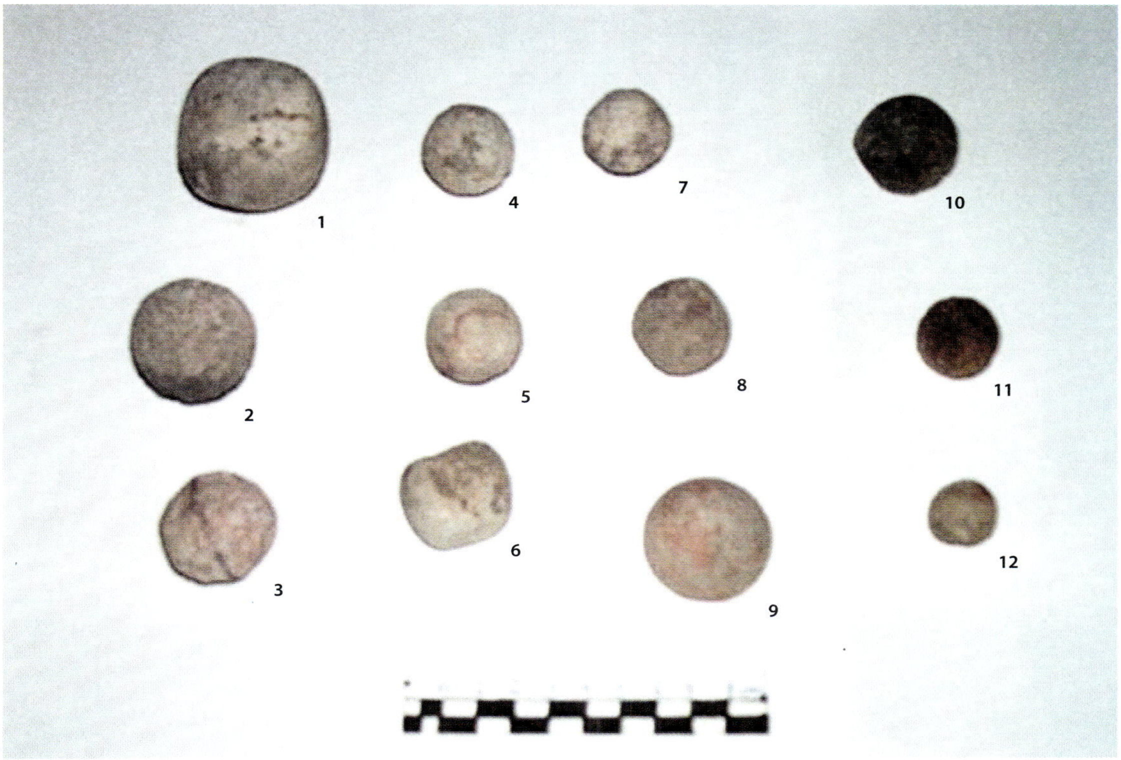

Figure 61 Stone balls from the Meham Block

Figure 62 Stone pestles from the Meham Block

Figure 63 Chert tools and object from the Meham Block

4 Chert blade of the Harappan period. From Farmana-1.

5 Chert blade of the Harappan period. From Farmana-1.

6 Chert blade of the Harappan period. From Kheri Meham.

7 Chert weight of the Harappan period. From Farmana-1.

8 Chert blade of the Harappan period. From Kheri Meham.

9 Chert blade of the Harappan period. From Kheri Meham.

10 Chert blade of the Harappan period. From Girawad-2.

COPPER OBJECTS

In the course of exploration, some copper objects were also collected from different sites. Most of them belong to the Harappan period. Almost all of them were badly corroded; the corrosion is visible on them. A brief description of these objects is given below.

DESCRIPTION OF ILLUSTRATED SPECIMENS

Figures 64 and 65

1 Copper spearhead of the Harappan period. From Farmana-1. (Figure 64-1 and Figure 65)

2 Copper socketed arrowhead of the Harappan period. From Girawad-2.

3 Copper chisel of the Harappan period. From Girawad-2.

4 Fragment of copper chisel of the Harappan period. From Girawad-2.

5 Fragment of copper objects of the Harappan period. From Farmana-1.

6 Fragment of copper objects of the Harappan period. From Farmana-1.

7 Fragment of a copper arrowhead of the Harappan period. From Girawad-2.

8 Fragment of unidentified copper object of the

Figure 64 Copper objects from the Meham Block

Figure 65 Copper spearhead from the Meham Block

Figure 66 Gold and bone objects from the Meham Block

Harappan period. From Girawad-2.

9 Fragment of unidentified copper object of Harappan period. From Girawad-2.

GOLD OBJECTS

During the exploration, some gold objects were found from the site Gurawer-2. A detailed description of the illustrated objects is as follows.

DESCRIPTION OF ILLUSTRATED SPECIMENS

Figure 66

1 Gold pendent (?) of the Harappan period, having weight about 2.5 g. From Girawad-2.

2 Gold object of the Harappan period. From Girawad-2.

3 Bone pendent of the PGW period, having holes for putting string and incised decoration. From Madina-2.

BEADS

Beads of semi-precious stones, such as carnelian, agate, jasper, faience, shell and steatite, were the part of the jewelry worn by the people of ancient times. Beads of terracotta and steatite, which are more numerous and with great variety in shape, must have been worn by poorer people. Beads of metal such as copper, gold and silver were also made.

In the course of explorations conducted by the researcher, beads of semi-precious stones, such as carnelian, agate, faience, jasper, terracotta, shell and ivory were collected from various sites. These beads are very beautiful and attractive in therir shape and appearance. A brief description of illustrated beads is as below.

DESCRIPTION OF ILLUSTRATED SPECIMENS

Figure 67

1 Etched carnelian bead of the Late Harappan

Figure 67 Beads from the Meham Block

period. From Madina-2.

2 Carnelian beads of the Harappan period, long barrel biconical. From Farmana-1.

3 Carnelian bead of the Harappan period, barrel shaped. From Seman-1.

4 Carnelian bead of the Late Harappan period. From Ajaib-2.

5 Etched carnelian bead of the Harappan period, elliptical shape. From Farmana-1.

6 Terracotta cylindrical bead of the Harappan period. From Farmana-1.

7 Agate beads of the Harappan period, long barrel on plan and lenticular in section. From Farmana-1.

8 Agate bead of the Harappan period, long-barrel-shaped. From Farmana-1.

9 Agate bead of the Late Harappan period, triangular in shape. From Madina-2.

10 Faience bead of the Harappan period, standard biconical plan and circular section. From Kheri Meham.

11 Faience bead of the Harappan period, ring-shaped. From Kheri Meham.

12 Faience bead of the Late Harappan period. From Girawad-2.

13 Faience bead of the Late Harappan period, barrel-shaped. From Farmana-3.

14 Faience cylindrical bead of the Harappan period. From Kheri Meham.

15 Agate bead of the Harappan period, cylindrical in shape, having etched circles. From Farmana-1.

16 Faience bead of the Late Harappan period, cylindrical shape. From Seman-1.

17 Faience bead of the Harappan period, cylindrical shape. From Seman-1.

18 Faience bead of the Late Harappan period, cylindrical shape. From Seman-1.

19 Agate bead of the Late Harappan period, cylindrical in shape. From Bahelba-2.

20 Faience bead of the Late Harappan period, cylindrical in shape. From Seman-1.

Figure 68 Beads and disc from the Meham Block

Figure 68

1 Shell bead of the Harappan period, disc-shaped. From Farmana-1.

2 Steatite bead of the Harappan period, disc-shaped.From Kheri-Meham.

3 Steatite bead of the Harappan period, disc-shaped. From Girawad-2.

10 Agate bead of the Late Harappan period, short-barrel-shaped. From Madina-2.

11-12 Steatite beads of the Harappan period, disc-shaped. From Seman-1.

13 Shell micro-bead of the Early Harappan period, cylindrical shape. From Farmana-1.

14-18 Steatite micro-bead of the Harappan period, disc-shaped. From Farmana-1.

19 Carnelian bead of the Harappan period, barrel-shaped. From Seman-1.

20-22 Steatite bead of the Harappan period, disc-shaped. From Girawad-2.

23-27 Steatite micro-bead of the Harappan period, disc-shaped. From Girawad-2.

28 Faience bead of the Late Harappan period, barrel-shaped, decorated with oblique stroke. From Bahelba-3.

29-30 Steatite micro-bead of the Harappan period, disc-shaped. From Farmana-1.

31-36 Steatite micro-beads of the Harappan period, disc-shaped. From Farmana-1.

37 Faience bead of the Late Harappan period, cylindrical shape. From Seman-1.

38-43 Steatite micro-bead of the Harappan period, disc-shaped. From Kheri Meham.

44 Steatite bead of the Early Harappan period, disc-shaped. From Mokhra-3.

45-46 Statite micro-bead of the Harappan period. From Kheri Meham.

47 Statite bead of the Harappan period, cylindrical shape. From Farmana-1.

48-49 Steatite micro-bead of the Harappan period, disc-shaped. From Girawad-2.

50 Shell micro-bead of the Harappan period. From Seman-1.

51-55 Steatite micro-beads of the Harappan period. From Farmana-1.

56 Shell micro-bead of the Harappan period. From Girawad-2.

57 Faience bead of the Late Harappan period, mildly gadrooned. From Kheri Meham.

58 Steatite bead of the Harappan period, rectangular in shape. From Seman-1.

59 Steatite micro-bead of the Harappan period. From Farmana-1. It is so small in size that its hole is not visible by naked eyes. This gives an idea about the advanced technique of the Harappan bead making.

60-63 Steatite micro-bead of the Harappan period. From Girawad-2.

64 Steatite bead of the Harappan period, disc-shaped. From Seman-1.

65-66 Steatite micro-bead of the Harappan period. From Farmana-1.

67 Crystal disc of the Late Harappan period. From Madina-2.

BANGLES

Bangle is the most common type of jewellary worn by the women from the dawn of civilization. These bangles are made of gold, silver, copper, faience, terracotta, shell and glass. Terracotta and faience bangles are very common during the Harappan period, and shell bangles were also worn during this period. Faience bangles were made of blue vitreous paste, decorated on the outer side with incised design. The bangles were mostly round in shape, but some are slightly bent. Glass and shell bangles were very common during the Historical and Medieval periods. A few bangle pieces discovered from the area under study are described below.

DESCRIPTION OF ILLUSTRATED SPECIMENS

Figure 69

1 Fragment of a faience bangle of the Harappan period, plano-convex in section, sky blue in colour, decorated with oblique lines. From Farmana-1.

2 Fragment of faience bangle of the Late Harappan period, oblate in section, light blue with white glaze, decorated on exterior with horizontal line superimposed by a zigzag line. From Kheri Meham.

3 Fragment of a faience bangle of the Late Harappan period, flattened oblate section, light blue, decorated with oblique strokes dividing panels of horizontal lines enclosing oblique strokes. From Farmana-3.

4 Fragment of a faience bangle of the Late Harappan period, externally flattened section, light blue, decorated with criss-cross design between horizontal lines. From Kheri Meham.

5 Fragment of a faience bangle of the Late Harappan period, elliptical shaped, sky blue in colour. From Farmana-1.

6 Fragment of a faience bangle of the Late Harappan period, light blue in colour, decorated on exterior with chequered pattern. From Farmana-1.

7 Fragment of a faience bangle of the Late Harappan period, trianglular in section, light blue in colour, decorated with oblique lines on either side of the ridge forming the chevron pattern. From Madina-2.

8 Fragment of a faience bangle of the Late Harappan period. From Bahelba-3.

9-12 Fragment of a faience bangle of the Late Harappan period, circular in section. From Kheri Meham.

13-15 Fragment of a faience bangle of the Late Harappan period, heart-shaped, and light blue in colour. From Farmana-1.

16-17 Fragment of a faience bangle of the Harappan period, light blue, decorated with oblique strokes dividing panels of horizontal lines enclosing oblique strokes. From Girawad-2.

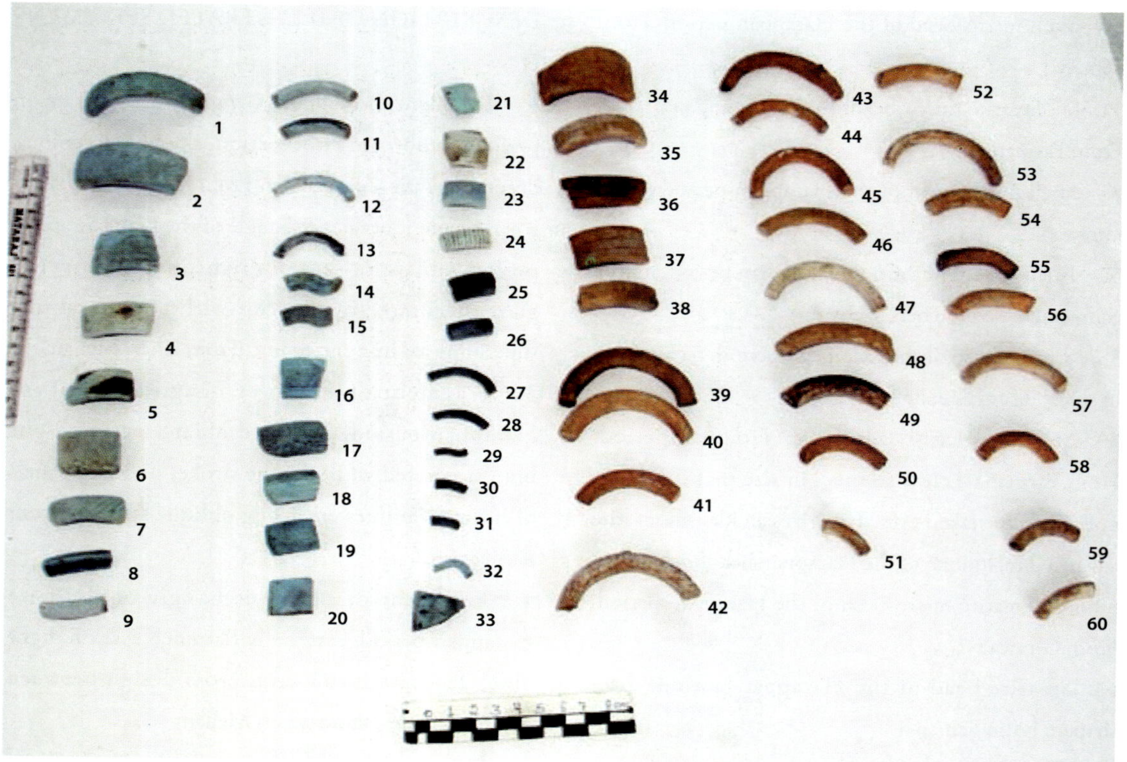

Figure 69 Faience and terracotta bangles from the Meham Block

18 Fragment of a faience bangle of the Late Harappan period. From Seman-5.

19-20 Fragment of a faience bangle of the Late Harappan period, bearing a mid-rib on the exterior. From Sekhpur-Titari.

21 Fragment of a faience bangle of the Late Harappan period. From Ganganagar-1.

22 Fragment of a faience bangle of the Late Harappan period, externally corrugated. The ridges are decorated with chevron design. From Kharkhra-1.

23-24 Fragment of a faience bangle of the Late Harappan period, plano-concave in section, decorated with oblique lines. From Farmana-3.

25 Fragment of a faience bangle of the Late Harappan period, dark green, decorated with oblique lines. From Seman-1.

26 Fragment of a faience bangle of the Late Harappan period, dark green, decorated with oblique lines. From Seman-1.

27-31 Fragment of a faience bangle of the Late Harappan period, thin heart-shaped, dark blue in colour. From Farmana-1.

32 Fragment of a faience bangle of the Late Harappan period, dark blue in colour. From Madina-2.

33 Fragment of a faience bangle of the Harappan period, light blue in colour, decorated on exterior with a chequered pattern giving an impression of square design. From Farmana-2.

34 Fragment of a terracotta bangle of the Harappan period, made of three loops joined together. From Farmana-1.

35 Fragment of a terracotta bangle of the Harappan period, made of two loops joined together. From Girawad-2.

36 Fragment of a terracotta bangle the Harappan period, made of three loops joined together. From Kheri Meham.

37 Fragment of a terracotta bangle of the Harappan period, three loops joined together. From Kheri

Meham.

38 Fragment of a terracotta bangle of the Harappan period, made of two loops joined together, square in section. From Seman-1.

39-42 Fragment of a terracotta bangle of the Harappan period, of brick red core. From Farmana-1.

43-46 Fragment of a terracotta bangle of the Harappan period, of brick red core. From Seman-1.

47 Fragment of a terracotta bangle of the Harappan period, pink in colour. From Farmana-1.

48-51 Fragment of a terracotta bangle of the Harappan period, brick red core. From Kheri Meham.

52-57 Fragment of a terracotta bangle of the Harappan period. From Girawad-2.

58 Fragment of a terracotta bangle of the Harappan period. From Seman-6.

59 Fragment of a terracotta bangle of the Harappan period. From Farmana-3.

60 Fragment of a terracotta bangle of the Harappan period. From Farmana-1.

CHAPTER VI

STUDY OF COINS AND INSCRIPTION

A large number of coins have been found in exploration and excavation. In some cases, hundreds of these have been found in a single hoard. Some coins fell in the hands of greedy persons and were melted for their metal, others fortunately come in the hands of scholars for research. Numismatics is undoubtedly one of the most valuable sources of history. It, at times, confirms the information culled from other sources and by themselves provides information not known from other sources. Of about 40 Indo-Greek rulers, epigraphs refers to only a few and literature refers to half a dozen of them. The historicity of the rest of them are known only from coins, and after careful and patient study of these coins, numismatists attempt to establish chronology of kings and throw light on various aspects of their history on culture. Thus coins throw light on various aspects of the Indian history, such a political, economic, and social.

During the exploration in the area, the researcher discovered a large number of coins. These include a hoard of Kushana coins, containing 68 copper coins, two coins of the Yaudheyas, coins of the Sultanate period and also of the Mughal period. These are described in the following pages.

COINS OF THE KUSHANA

A hoard of 68 copper coin was found from Madina-4, which were buried in a bowl of the Kushana period. These coins are in a very good condition and belong to a later Kushana king Vasudeva II. The details of this hoard is as below (Figures 70-81).

Coin no. 1

Weight: 6.5788 g

Size: 22 mm

Shape: Circular

Obverse: King standing wearing a long coat. Putting oblation with his right hand at an alter.

Reverse: Shiva standing beside a bull, right hand resting on the horns of the bull. The face of Shiva is out of flane.

Coin no. 2

Weight: 4.6106 g

Size: 18 mm

Shape: Circular

Obverse: Same as Coin no. 1

Reverse: Same as Coin no.1

Coin no. 3

Weight: 4.6106 g

Size: 18 mm

Shape: Circular

Obverse: Same as Coin no. 1

Reverse: Same as Coin no.1

Coin no. 4

Weight: 4.9960 g

Size: 19 mm

Shape: Circular

Obverse: Same as Coin no. 1

Reverse: Shiva standing besides a bull, holding a trident in his left hand, his right hand resting on the horns of bull.

Coin no. 5

Weight: 5.7875 g

Size: 21 mm

Shape: Circular

Figure 70 Kushana coins from Madina-4

Figure 71 Kushana coins from Madina-4

Obverse: Same as Coin no. 1

Reverse: Same as Coin no.1. But the face of Shiva is out of flane.

Coin no. 6

Weight: 5.9865 g

Size: 19.5 mm

Shape: Circular

Obverse: King standing wearing a long coat and boots. Putting incense with his right hand at an alter.

Reverse: Same as Coin no.4

Coin no. 7

Weight: 5.2112 g

Size: 18 mm

Shape: Circular

Obverse: Same as Coin no. 1

Reverse: Same as Coin no. 1

Coin no. 8

Weight: 5.8615 g

Size: 20 mm

Shape: Circular

Obverse: Same as Coin no. 1

Reverse: Same as Coin no.1

Coin no. 9

Weight: 5.1665 g

Size: 20 mm

Shape: Circular

Obverse: Same as Coin no. 1

Reverse: Same as Coin no.1

Coin no. 10

Weight: 4.4965 g

Size: 20 mm

Shape: Circular

Obverse: Same as Coin no.1

Reverse: Same as Coin no.1

Coin no. 11

Weight: 6.0826 g

Size: 20 mm

Shape: Circular

Obverse: Same as Coin no.1.

Reverse: Same as Coin no.1.

Coin No. 12

Weight: 5.8460 g

Size: 22 mm

Shape: Circular

Obverse: Same as Coin no. 1

Reverse: Same as Coin no. 1

Coin No. 13

Weight: 6.2489 g

Size: 20 mm

Shape: Circular

Obverse: King standing wearing a long coat and trousers. Putting incense with his right hand at an alter.

Reverse: Shiva standing besides a bull, wearing a *dhoti*, holding *tamgha* (?) in his right hand.

Coin no. 14

Weight: 4.4751 g

Size: 20 mm

Shape: Circular

Obverse: Same as Coin no. 1

Reverse: Same as Coin no. 6

Coin no. 15

Weight: 4.8395 g

Size: 19 mm

Shape: Circular

Obverse: Same as Coin no. 1

Reverse: Same as Coin no. 1

Coin no. 16

Weight: 4.127 g

Size: 19.5 mm

Figure 72 Kushana coins from Madina-4

Figure 73 Kushana coins from Madina-4

Shape: Circular
Obverse: King standing wearing a long coat and boots. Putting oblation with his right hand at an alter. The head of king is out of flane.
Reverse: Shiva standing beside a bull.

Coin no. 17
Weight: 5.9701 g
Size: 19.5 mm
Shape: Circular
Obverse: Same as Coin no. 1
Reverse: Same as Coin no. 1

Coin no. 18
Weight: 5.4106 g
Size: 20 mm
Shape: Circular
Obverse: Same as Coin no. 1
Reverse: Same as Coin no. 1

Coin no. 19
Weight: 3.8482 g
Size: 1.7 mm
Shape: Circular
Obverse: King standing wearing a long coat and trousers. Putting alteration with his right hand at an alter.
Reverse: Same as Coin no.1

Coin no. 20
Weight: 5.6469 g
Size: 20 mm
Shape: Circular
Obverse: Same as Coin no. 1
Reverse: Same as Coin no. 1. The Face of Bull and Shiva are out of flane.

Coin no. 21
Weight: 5.5298 g
Size: 20 mm
Shape: Circular
Obverse: Same as Coin no.1
Reverse: Same as Coin no.1

Coin no. 22
Weight: 5.4579 g
Size: 21.5 mm
Shape: Circular
Obverse: King standing wearing a long coat and trousers. Putting oblation with his right hand at an alter.
Reverse: Same as Coin no. 1

Coin no. 23
Weight: 5.5572 g
Size: 19 mm
Shape: Circular
Obverse: Same as Coin no. 1
Reverse: Same as Coin no. 1

Coin no. 24
Weight: 5.4643 g
Size: 20 mm
Shape: Circular
Obverse: Same as Coin no. 1
Reverse: Same as Coin no. 1

Coin no. 25
Weight: 5.7869 g
Size: 20 mm
Shape: Circular
Obverse: Same as Coin no. 1
Reverse: Same as Coin no. 1

Coin no. 26
Weight: 5.9904 g
Size: 18.5 mm
Shape: Circular
Obverse: Same as Coin no.1
Reverse: Same as Coin no.1. But Shiva is wearing a *dhoti*.

Figure 74 Kushana coins from Madina-4

Figure 75 Kushana coins from Madina-4

Coin no. 27
Weight: 6.5514 g
Size: 20 mm
Shape: Circular
Obverse: Same as Coin no. 1
Reverse: Same as Coin no. 1

Coin no. 28
Weight: 5.5423 g
Size: 21 mm
Shape: Irregular
Obverse: Same as Coin no. 1
Reverse: Same as Coin no. 1

Coin no. 29
Weight: 5.0867 g
Size: 25 mm
Shape: Circular
Obverse: Same as Coin no.1
Reverse: Same as Coin no.1

Coin no. 30
Weight: 5.8788 g
Size: 19.5 mm
Shape: Circular
Obverse: Same as Coin no. 1. But the face of king is out of flane.
Reverse: Same as Coin No.1. But the face of bull and Shiva are out of flane.

Coin no. 31
Weight: 5.8886 g
Size: 21 mm
Shape: Circular
Obverse: Same as Coin no. 1
Reverse: Same as Coin no.1

Coin no. 32
Weight: 5.294 g
Size: 21 mm
Shape: Circular
Obverse: Same as Coin no.1. But the king is wearing trousers.
Reverse: Same as Coin no. 1

Coin no. 33
Weight: 5.4261 g
Size: 19.5 mm
Shape: Rectangular
Obverse: Same as Coin no. 1
Reverse: Same as Coin no. 1

Coin no. 34
Weight: 7.9777 g
Size: 20 mm
Shape: Circular
Obverse: King standing wearing a long coat, having a halo and holding a trident to right.
Reverse: Same as Coin no.1

Coin no. 35
Weight: 7.7988 g
Size: 20 mm
Shape: Circular
Obverse: Same as Coin no. 34
Reverse: Same as Coin no. 1.

Coin no. 36
Weight: 4.6805 g
Size: 19 mm
Shape: Circular
Obverse: Same as Coin no. 1. But the king has a halo.
Reverse: Same as Coin no. 1. But the face of Shiva and bull are out of flane.

Coin no. 37
Weight: 5.5293 g
Size: 20 mm
Shape: Circular
Obverse: Same as Coin no. 1
Reverse: Same as Coin no. 1

Figure 76 Kushana coins from Madina-4

Figure 77 Kushana coins from Madina-4

Coin no. 38
Weight: 5.5293 g
Size: 20 mm
Shape: Circular
Obverse: Same as Coin no. 1
Reverse: Same as Coin no. 1. But the face of Shiva and bull are out of flane.

Coin no. 39
Weight: 4.3406 g
Size: 18 mm
Shape: Circular
Obverse: Same as Coin no. 1
Reverse: Same as Coin no. 1

Coin no. 40
Weight: 4.5412 g
Size: 17 mm
Shape: Circular
Obverse: Same as Coin no. 1
Reverse: Same as Coin no. 1

Coin no. 41
Weight: 6.8721 g
Size: 19.1 mm
Shape: Circular
Obverse: Same as Coin no. 1. But the king has a halo.
Reverse: Same as Coin no. 1. But Shiva has a trident in his left hand.

Coin no. 42
Weight: 5.7599 g
Size: 19 mm
Shape: Round
Obverse: Same as Coin no. 1
Reverse: Same as Coin no. 1

Coin no. 43
Weight: 4.7591 g
Size: 20 mm
Shape: Circular
Obverse: Same as Coin no.1
Reverse: Same as Coin no. 1

Coin no. 44
Weight: 5.8686 g
Size: 20.5 mm
Shape: Circular
Obverse: Same as Coin no. 1
Reverse: Same as Coin no. 1

Coin no. 45
Weight: 8.4854 g
Size: 24 mm
Shape: Circular
Obverse: King standing having a halo. Wearing a long coat and trousers. Putting oblation with his right hand at an alter, holding a trident in left hand.
Reverse: Shiva standing with a bull, having a halo. Right hand resting on the horns of bull, holding a trident in left hand.

Coin no. 46
Weight: 4.7951 g
Size: 18 mm
Shape: Circular
Obverse: Same as Coin no. 1
Reverse: Same as Coin no. 1

Coin no. 47
Weight: 4.2965 g
Size: 18 mm
Shape: Irregular
Obverse: Same as Coin no. 1
Reverse: Same as Coin no. 1

Coin no. 48
Weight: 4.4997 g
Size: 18 mm
Shape: Circular
Obverse: Same as Coin no.1
Reverse: Same as Coin no.1

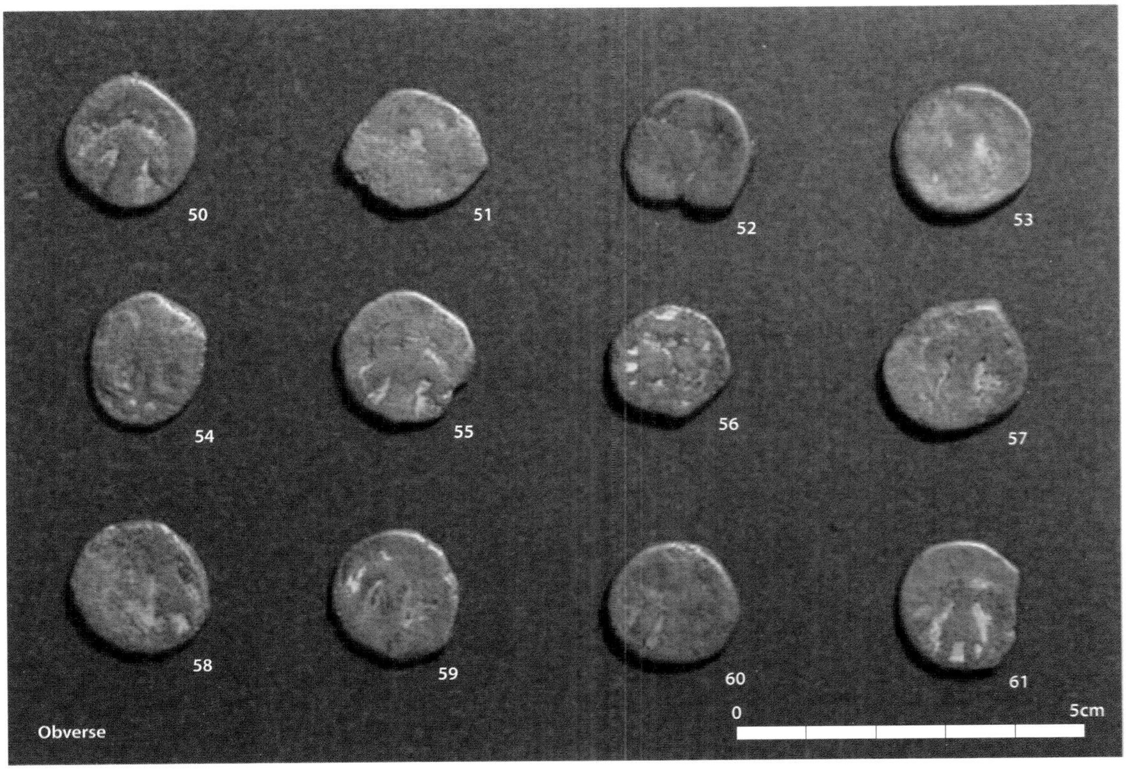

Figure 78 Kushana coins from Madina-4

Figure 79 Kushana coins from Madina-4

Coin no. 49
Weight: 5.4812 g
Size: 20 mm
Shape: Circular
Obverse: Same as Coin no. 1
Reverse: Same as Coin no. 1

Coin no. 50
Weight: 6.0747 g
Size: 19.5 mm
Shape: Circular
Obverse: King standing wearing a long coat. Holding a trident, putting oblation with his right hand at an alter.
Reverse: Shiva standing besides a bull. Having a halo, holding a trident in his left hand and a diadem, *tamgha* (?) in his right hand.

Coin no. 51
Weight: 5.4812 g
Size: 18.5 mm
Shape: Circular
Obverse: Same as Coin no. 1
Reverse: Same as Coin no. 1

Coin no. 52
Weight: 6.05734 g
Size: 18.5 mm
Shape: Circular
Obverse: Same as Coin no. 1
Reverse: Same as Coin no. 1

Coin no. 53
Weight: 5.0897 g
Size: 20 mm
Shape: Circular
Obverse: Same as Coin no. 1
Reverse: Same as Coin no. 1

Coin no. 54
Weight: 4.381gm
Size: 20 mm
Shape: Circular
Obverse: Same as Coin no. 1
Reverse: Same as Coin no. 1

Coin no. 55
Weight: 5.760 g
Size: 19 mm
Shape: Circular
Obverse: Same as Coin no. 1
Reverse: Same as Coin no. 1

Coin no. 56
Weight: 4.6988 g
Size: 16.6 mm
Shape: Circular
Obverse: Same as Coin no. 1
Reverse: Same as Coin no. 1

Coin no. 57
Weight: 4.9593 g
Size: 21 mm
Shape: Circular
Obverse: Same as Coin no. 1
Reverse: Same as Coin no. 1

Coin no. 58
Weight: 5.9332 g
Size: 20 mm
Shape: Circular
Obverse: Same as Coin no. 1
Reverse: Same as Coin no.1. But the face of Shiva is out of flane.

Coin no. 59
Weight: 4.8587 g
Size: 19 mm
Shape: Circular
Obverse: Same as Coin no. 1
Reverse: Same as Coin no. 1

Figure 80 Kushana coins from Madina-4

Figure 81 Kushana coins from Madina-4

Coin no. 60
Weight: 6.4100 g
Size: 19 mm
Shape: Circular
Obverse: Same as Coin no. 1
Reverse: Same as Coin no. 1

Coin no. 61
Weight: 4.6062 g
Size: 19 mm
Shape: Circular
Obverse: Same as Coin no. 1
Reverse: Same as Coin no. 1

Coin no. 62
Weight: 5.4668 g
Size: 19.5 mm
Shape: Irregular
Obverse: Same as Coin no. 1
Reverse: Same as Coin no. 1

Coin no. 63
Weight: 4.1744 g
Size: 19 mm
Shape: Circular
Obverse: Same as Coin no. 1
Reverse: Same as Coin no. 1

Coin no. 64
Weight: 4.2231 g
Size: 20 mm
Shape: Circular
Obverse: Same as Coin no. 1
Reverse: Same as Coin no. 1

Coin no. 65
Weight: 6.0212 g
Size: 20 mm
Shape: Circular
Obverse: Same as Coin no. 1
Reverse: Same as Coin no. 1

Coin no. 66
Weight: 4.6918 g
Size: 18.5 mm
Shape: Circular
Obverse: Same as Coin no. 1
Reverse: Same as Coin no. 1

Coin no. 67
Weight: 6.4181 g
Size: 20 mm
Shape: Circular
Obverse: King standing wearing a long coat and trousers, and having a trident behind his right hand. Putting oblation with his right hand at an alter.
Reverse: Same as Coin no.1. But the face of Shiva is out of flane.

Coin no. 68
Weight: 5.3711 g
Size: 19 mm
Shape: Circular
Obverse: Same as Coin no. 1
Reverse: Same as Coin no. 1

COINS OF THE YAUDHEYAS

During the exploration, the author found two Yaudheyas coin from the site of Farmana-3. These coins were in a good state of preservation when found and have been chemical treated and conserved. Both of the coins belong to c. third - fourth centuries ACE (Variety b) and are of Yaudheyas ganasya jaya. Scholars have divergent views about the words *dvi*, which is the shorter form of *dvitiya*. While A. Cunningham considered *dvi* as referring to the second division of the tribe, V. Smith took them to refer to the second section of the tribe. Jai Prakash holds the word *dvi* to refer to the second mint of the Yaudheyas. But his theory has been contradicted by the discovery of more than 30,000 coin moulds of the Yaudheyas during the excavation at Sunet (*IAR* 1983-84). Where

Figure 82 Yaudheya and Medieval coins

Figure 83 Yaudheya and Medieval coins

all the types of coin moulds of the Yaudheyas were found together. Swami Omanand Saraswati holds the view that the Yaudheyas defeated the Kushana thrice. After the first victory, they issue the coins with the legend Yaudheyas ganasya jaya, while after the second victory they added the word *dvi.* After the third win, they put *tri* with legend (*Ancient mints of Haryana*). The description of both coins is as given blow.

Coin no.1

Plates no. 82 (Obverse) and Plate no. 83 (Reverse)

Metal: Copper

Size: 24 mm

Weight: 10.8219 g

Shape: Circular

Provenance: Farmana-3

Die: obverse: 22.5 mm; Reverse: 20 mm

Obverse: Karttikeya standing facing holding a spear in his right hands and his left hand resting on his hip. A peacock stands near his left foot.

Brahmi legend:

From 1' to 40' clock: Yaudheya ga

From 7' to 10' clock: nasya jaya

Between head and spear: dvi

Reverse: Female deity in tribhang mudra with her right hand raised and her left hand resting on her hip. Border of dots. Flower pots are placed to the left of the deity and a nandipada to the right.

Coin no.2

Plate no. 82 (obverse) and Plate no. 83 (Reverse)

Metal: Copper

Size: 25 mm

Weight: 10.9712 g

Shape: Circular

Provenance: Farmana-3

Die: obverse: 22.5 mm; Reverse: 20 mm

Obverse: Karttikeya standing holding a spear in his right hand and his left hand resting on his hip. A peacock stands near his left foot.

Brahmi legend:

From 1' to 40' clock: Yaudheya ga

From 7' to 10' clock: nasya jaya

Between head and spear: dvi

Reverse: Female deity in tribhang mudra with her right hand raised and her left resting on her hip. Border of dots. Flower pots are placed to the left of the deity and a nandipada to the right.

MEDIEVAL COINS

Four medieval coins were found from the study region. These coins belong to the 13th to 17th centuries ACE and are issued by Muhammad Tughlaq and Sikander Saha Lodhi. These are described below.

Coin no.5

Plate no. 82 (obverse) and Plate no. 83 (Reverse)

Metal: Copper

Shape: Circular

Size: 22 mm

Weight: 11.1277 g

Provenance: Bedwa-2

Obverse: Inside मनअत्ता उल सुल्तान फ़कद अत्ता अलरहमान Around circuramfance दर तख्तगाह देहली साल बर अफसद सी ।

Reverse: महर सद टंका रासजदर रोजगार, बंदा उम्मीदवार मोहम्मद तुगलक

Coin no.4

Plate no. 82 (obverse) and Plate no. 83 (Reverse)

Metal: Copper

Shope: Circular

Size: 17 mm

Weight: 8.6391 g

Provenance: Bedwa-2

Obverse: सिकन्दर शाह लोधी, फे जमन अलमोमनीन, अमीर खीलदल खलीफा ।

Reverse: अलहतुकल अली, अलरहमन, सिकन्दर शाह, बहलूलशाह सुलतान

Coin no.6

Plate no. 82 (obverse) and Plate no. 83 (Reverse)
Metal: Copper
Shape: Circular
Size: 1.95 mm
Weight: 9.3736 g
Provenance: Bedwa-2
Obverse: Same as Coin no. 4
Reverse: Same as Coin no. 4

Coin no.3

Plate no. 82 (obverse) and Plate no. 83 (Reverse)
Metal: Silver
Shape: Circular
Size: 22 mm
Weight: 11.010 g
Provenance: Girawad-2
Obverse: Mohammad Shah Badsha Gazi, Sahil-e-Quran Naz Mubariq
Reverse: Darul-khalifa zarus mimnal Maroos (1045 sana).

STUDY OF INSCRIPTION

Epigraphy is the study of inscriptions, and the 'Inscription' literally means any writing engraved on some objects. For the ancient and medieval periods of the Indian history, the study of inscription has a special importance. Of all such sources for the reconstruction of the Indian history, epigraphic records are the most important, for the provided material for the major part of what we know about the achievements of Indian people of the past.

In the area of present study, there are ten inscriptions reported by S.R. Phoghat. All these are in Persian. Do details of these inscription is as given below (Phoghat 1978). In this description, the persian scripts are replaced with the devanagari scripts.

Jamal Khan Tomb Inscription

A red sand-stone (14 × 10.5 inches) is fixed over the tomb of Jamal Khan bearing the following inscription:

बिसमिल्लाए रहमाने रहीम लाइला इलल्लाह मोहम्मद रसुलिल्लाह ।
दरअहदे दौलते सुलताने सलातीन जलालुदीन मोहम्मद अकबर
बादशाहे गाजी ।
मक़बुले रहमाने जमालखान बिन्ने मनसूर राउजा तौफिक याफ्त
रास्ता कननिद जमालखान रा उमीदे सवाब के
याबदमिन तारीख जिलक़ाद ह॰७ सन्ह् अलिफ दा मायतह् ।

It can be dated to H. 1100 (17th August, 1689 ACE).

Pirzada Mosque Inscription

छरअहदे हज़रते दौलते शाहनशाहे आलमपना जहिरूदीन मोहम्मदे
बाबुर ।
गजी बादद्याह खलदअल्लाह मुल्के वा सुलतान बनदए दरगाह मेहरी
।
अलफ़कीरे हकीर जनिओ सुनु आगा इब्न □ीख सुनु वा साकीने
हिसारे शाहमानी ।
बतौफिके अल्लाहताला तौफिकताफ्त मस्जिदे दर कस्बए महिमे रास
कनानिद हख ताला ।
मज़ाब बा मुस्ताब गरदान दू बमिने वा फज़ले बतारीखे पंजुमे माहे
रबिउल आवल सन्ह सत वा सुलसइने वा तसहिमायत ।

It can be dated to 7th November 1529 ACE.

Jain Masjid Inscription

दरअहदे दौलते सुलताने सलातीन जिलल्हा फिलआलमिन मरदे
सरीरे सलतनत ।
वा खिलाफा हजरते मोहम्मद हमायू□बादद्याहे गाज़ी खलदअल्लाह
मुल्के वा सुलताने व आलाहे अमरा वा सायाहे हज़रते मकबूले ।
दारइन...... सुलताने सरहिन्दएदीन गरिन्दए दरगाहेअमीर यादगारे
ताघाए बतौफ़िक अल्लाह ताला ।
तौक़ियाफ़त मस्जिदे जामे कस्बए महिम रास कनानिद अल्लाह ताला
मज़ाब वा मुस्ताब ।
गरदानत बमदद वा फज़लेह् वा कमाले करामे बतारीखे हफ़तुमे माहे
रज़ब सन्ह् सुबा वा सुलसाइने वा तसइमायते।

It can be dated to 7th Rajab 937 (24th February, 1531 ACE)."

Meham Mosque Inscription

छरअहदे दौलते शाहनशाहे आलमपना हज़रते मोहम्मद हमायू□
बादशाह ।
खलद अल्लाह वा मुल्के इमारते हाजाल मस्जिद तौफ़ीकयफ्त..........
..........कसावान कसबए महिमेरास कनानिद बतारीखे माहे सोबान

सन्ह असनी वा अरबाइनी वा तसइमायत

It can be dated to January 1536 ACE.

Oussayan Mosque Inscription

बिसमिल्लाए रहमाने रहीम इन्ना फतेनालक फतिहनमुबिना गुसादबाद
बाशादि हमेद्दाा इ□दरगाह सखु असहद अन लाइलाइलल्लाह
दरअहदे दौलते तन्दकह् हज़रते सुलेमानि ५ोरद्दाह हसनसूर
सुलतान तौफ़िक या त ाबिनाए इ□मस्तिद
दर मकामे दौलताबाद युसफ इब्न हसनसूर सैयदआलि दौलतखान
अउमीदे सबाबहदिसे नववीमिन एनिएमस्जिदन बनि अल्लाह ताला
लहु क़सरन फिल जत्रते वलजिनान अबका
अल्लाह ताला फिदुनियां वा वक्फ अल्लाह ताला अलल्अदले
वलअहसान फिलहादिवल असराइन मन शहरूल मुबारक अलमुक़र्रम
शहरे रमजान सन्ह नुसदचहल नुहबुद ह ७कि मोयसर रसानिद

It can be dated to 29th December, 1542 ACE.

Pirzada Mosque Inscriiption

छरअहदे दलिते हज़रते बन्दगानखिलाफते पनाह सुलतान
शाहबुदीन मोहम्मद साहिबे कुराने सानी शाहजान बादशाहे गाज़ी
खलद
खिलाफते अबदन तौफिकयाफ्त शेखनासिर इब्नद्दोख अल्हदाद माहमी
सन्ह अलिफ वा खुमसइनेवाअहद

It can be dated to AH 1051" [12th April, 1641 ACE].

Jami Mosque Inscription

छरअहदे सआदतेमहदेहद वा मदे जमीन
व जमान खदीव मकीन वा मकान सुलताने
स्लातीन जिल्लाहफिल आलमीन मोहम्मद औरंगजेब
बहदुरे आलमगीर बादद्दाहे गाज़ी खलदअल्लाह मुल्के
वा सुलताने तामीर मस्जिदे जामे कस्बएमहिम हस्बिल हुक्म अक्दस
बइतमामे बन्दए दरगाह ख्वाजा रहमत अल्लाह बइतमाम रसीद
अल्लाह ताला मुजाब वा मुस्तजाब गरदानाद बमिल्ले वा फजले
फिलतारीखे हफदहमे शहरे मोहर्रम उल हराम सन्हेसमान वा
सुबइन वा अलफ हिजरि वा सन्ह आसिर जलुसे मुबारक

It can be dated to 17th of the month Muharram, AH 1078 (9th July, 1667 ACE).

Classayan Mosque Inscription

बिसमिल्लाए रहमाने रहीम
दरअहदे दौलत वा जमान ह९७
जिल्लेसुबानी आबुल ज़फर
मुहियदीन मोहम्मद औरंगजेब
बादशाहेगाज़ी खलद अल्लाहमुल्के
वा सुलतान मस्जिदरा कसायान
जांहगीर ह९७....................
तरतीब करद् दर शहरे रमजान सन्ह तसईन व अलिफ

It can be dated to 6th October 1679 ACE.

Daula Khan inscription

बिसमिल्लाए रहमाने रहीम लाइलाहइल्लाह मोहम्मदरसुलल्लाह
या अल्लाह याफ़ता या मोहम्मद या नबीउल्ला
इ□इमारत ज़बैरे रब करीम बानियस दौलाखाने वाला शान
पिदरस बख़्तियारे नामवरे मुग़फिरते दस्तगाह दरियाखान
साले इतमामरा बअकल वा तमीज मस्जिदे मबिरा जखान बरख्वान

It can be dated to 31st July, 1696 ACE.

Daula Khan Inscription

बिसमिल्लाएरहमाने रहीम लाइला इलल्लाह मोहम्मद रसुलल्लाह
बन्दए दरगाए रहमानी ।
दौलाखालने मोहम्मदी मुरीदे गेलानी दानिस्तम के चाहार यार बर
हम इ□दुनिया हामा फानी तौफिकया त
दर हंगामे जिंइदगानी इ□मकबरा सार साख्त अज लुत्फे रबानी
दरअहदे औरंगजेब बादद्दाहे जिल्लेसुबहानी बैतारीखे शहरे रमजान
अलमुबारक सन्ह यकहजार वा यकसद वा चहारदह ह ७ हिज़रि
बइतमामे उस्ताद
आबु वलदे तैयब मेहमार,

It can be dated to AH 1114 (1703 ACE).

CHAPTER VII

CONCLUSION

HISTORY OF THE REGION

The antiquity of the Meham region can be traced back to the protohistoric period as is attested by the discovery of sites of this period. Archaeological explorations have revealed that the earliest inhabitants of this region belongs to pre-Harappan culture or Hakra Ware Culture whose remains have been discovered at three sites (Farmana-1, Kheri Meham-1, Girawad-2). This pottery shows some similarities with the pottery recovered from Choliathan (Mughal 1997: 86), Kunal (Khatri and Acharya 1995: 84-86). The excavation at Bhirrana threw a good light on this culture in the region (Rao *et al.* 2004: 61). Settlers of this culture at Bhirrana live in the dwelling pits. Along the edges of these pits post-holes have been noted. This type of dwelling pit was also recovered from Kunal as well (Khatri and Acharya 1995: 84-85). People of this culture used both handmade and wheel-made pottery. C14 dates available from Bhirrana (Rao *et al.* 2004: 66-67) and Kunal (Lal 1997: 84) put the chronological horizon of this culture between 4500 BCE to 3016 BCE. The question still unsolved is that this agriculture community was indigenous or migrated from somewhere else.

Second phase in the history of the region is represented by the people of Early Harappan period. People of the Hakra culture made technological development towards the first urbanization in the Indian subcontinent. Excavations at Bhirrana (Rao *et al.* 2004: 61) and Kunal (Khatri and Acharya 1995: 85) proved that there was no cultural break between the Hakra Culture and the Early Harappan Culture. There are eight sites in this region which belong to the Early Harappan period (Bahelba-2, Farmana-1, Farmana-3, Girawad-2, Kheri Meham-1, Mokhra-3, Seman-1 and Bahelba-2). Although there is not even a single excavated site in this region, some idea can be gathered from the excavated evidence of the neighbouring sites, such as Bhirrana, Kunal and

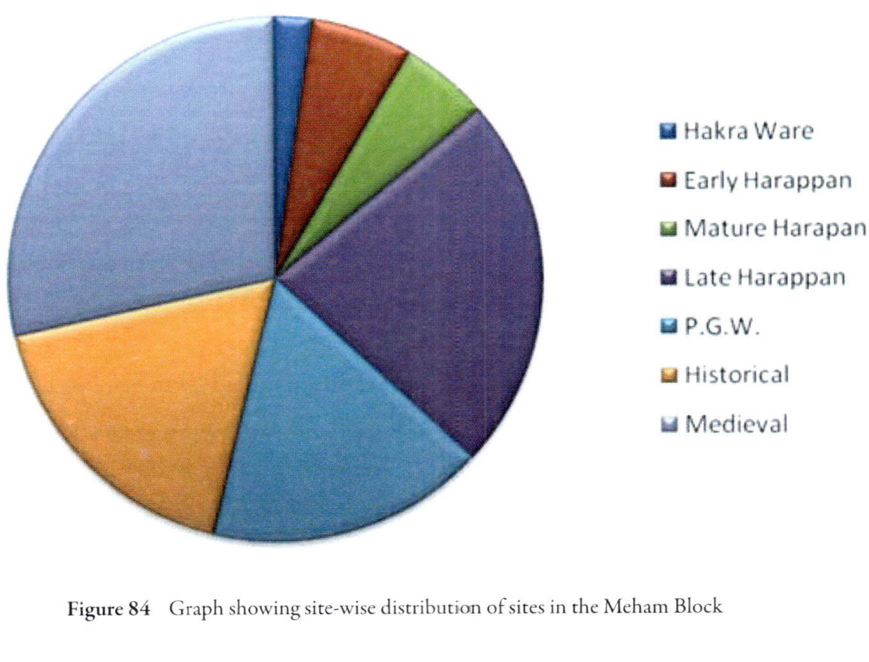

Figure 84 Graph showing site-wise distribution of sites in the Meham Block

Banawali.

The evidence obtained from these excavated sites shows that the Early Harappan people built their houses from mud bricks with thatched roofs. The Early Harappan settlements at Banawali (Bisht 1982: 113-24) and Kalibangan (Lal 1998: 21) were found to be fortified. Bricks used in the Early Harappan levels were in the ratio 3:2:1(30 cm × 20 cm × 10 cm), which is a typical feature of the Early Harappan times in the Ghaggar valley. The potters of this time were skilled in producing pottery with a wide range of shapes and decoration. Pottery is mainly wheel-made but a few examples of handmade pottery are noteworthy. All the six fabrics of Kalibangan were found during exploration at Early Harappan sites in this area. People of this period used copper tools, such as arrowhead, fishhook, celts and axes.

The economy of this period totally depend on agriculture, however trade was also a part of their economic activities. The discoveries of ploughed field from Kalibangan (Bisht 1982: 13) and terracotta plough from Banawali (Lal 1998: 61) give an idea about the farming technology during this period. The field of Kalibangan had two sets of furrows; one runs from north to south and the other from east to west. The distance between the individual furrows in the former was 1.9 m, whereas in the latter it was only 30 cm. It is the most interesting that this type of pattern of ploughing fields is still prevalent in the region. Toy cart frame and bull figurine give an idea about the type of transportation. The presence of copper, agate, gold and lapis lazuli in this area where the raw material source was not available tells us about their trade link with other areas. Seals found from the Early Harappan levels at Kunal (Khatri and Acharya 1995: 85) also indirectly give evidence of trade. Graffiti marks found on potsherds indicate the efforts of people to learn writing towards the later phase of this period.

The third phase in the history of the region is marked by the advent of the Mature Harappan civilization. Their settlements were discovered at Farmana-1, Farmana-3, Girawad-2, Kheri Meham-1 and Seman-1 in the area under present study. The excavations at Bhirrana and Kunal prove that the Harappan Civilization was totally indigenous. There is no cultural break between the Early Harappan and Mature Harappan phases at Bhirrana. The excavator has tried to prove that there was a transitory phase towards the Mature Harappan (Rao *et al.* 2004: 62). These people were versatile in town planning and fortified townships on classical "chess-board pattern" whose striking features were streets, defence walls and sanitary arrangements. They used well-fired pottery and the food includes wheat, barley, mustard, meat, fish, milk and milk products. Their seals are an indication of expert craftsmanship and the trade links with the contemporary western civilization. Their cubical and gamesman-type weight made of stone and ivory show a high degree of precision. Their skill in metallurgy is evident from a number of excavated materials.

In the region of the Ghaggar Valley, Rakhigarhi is the largest Harappan site and may have been the provincial capital. It is about 35 km northwest of Meham. In the adjoining region, Kalibangan (Lal 1998: 12-27), Siswal(Suraj Bhan 1975: 103-109), Banawali (Bisht 1982: 113-24), Kunal (Khatri and Acharya 1995: 84-86), Bhirrana (Rao *et al.* 2004: 60-68), Rakhigarhi (Nath 1997-98: 39-45), Mitathal (Suraj Bhan 1975: 23-32) and Balu (*IAR* 1979-80: 31-32) are the excavated Harappan sites, which have given details about this great civilization. The dried up of the Ghaggar River was the main cause for the decline of the Harappan civilization in the region.

Fourth phase in the protohistory of the region is distinguished by the late phase of the Harappan Culture and it can be assigned to the period between 1700 BCE - 1500 BCE. The density of villages in the region during this period increased, whereas in the Mature Harappan period there are only seven sites. The number of sites which belong to this period is 30 including two burial sites in this region. In absence of excavated site in this region, we have to depend upon other excavated sites like Daulatpur (*IAR* 1968-69: 8-9, 1976-77: 19), Banwali (Bisht 1982: 113-24), Balu (*IAR* 1979-80: 31-32) and Sanauli (Sharma et al. 2004: 35-44) and Mitathal (Suraj Bhan 1975).The houses of the Late Harappan period were made of mud bricks or robbed bricks from the earlier culture. The people related to the Late Harappan period lived in mud brick houses having a rammed earth foundation. The excavation at Bhagwanpura revealed that the Late Harappan people raised a mud platforms in two successive phases to get the higher area due to the fear of flood water of the Ghaggar River (Joshi 1993). At Mirzapur (Singh 1977), several mud-brick walls running diagonally in the trenches were partially exposed. A structural complex of mud brick walls consisted of two rooms. The excavation at Daulatpur (*IAR* 1976-77: 13-14) has also revealed the existence of post-holes, mud brick walls and half-baked bricks of different sizes which suggest different types of building activities during this period. The oval-shaped ovens have also been reported from Daulatpur.

The ceramic assemblage of this period seems to be a mixture of diverse ceramic traditions, such as the Early Harappan, Harappan, Bara and Cemetery H pottery. Some pottery shapes of this period seem to have evolved from the Mature Harappan period. But typical shapes of the Mature Harappan period were out of use. People of this period used mainly sturdy red ware, which is made of well-levitated clay and well fired. They are painted in black with linear, geometrical designs, floral and fauna. The main shapes are dish, bowl, storage jar, basin, dish-on-stand and vase. Bangles and beads of faience, pottery discs, beads of semi-precious stone, stone balls, terracotta toy cart frame and wheels and copper objects are among the antiquities of this period.

The excavation at Daulatpur (*IAR* 1976-77: 19) has the evidence of charred grains, semi-precious stone beads and copper objects, giving an idea about the economic life of the Late Harappan period. The sources of raw material like agate, carnelian and copper are not found locally or near the site. This suggests that these objects were bought here through trade. Besides trade, farming and hunting was the base of the Late Harappan economy. The cemetery found at Bedwa-2 and Bhaini Bharo-3 has given informations on the funeral process during this period. The bodies were laid in the north-south direction with the head towards north and near the head grave goods (pottery) were placed. Normally four pots of different size, that is, bowls, dish-on-stand with a long stem and *lota*-shaped pots were placed.

The excavation at Bhagwanpura has thrown a new light on the relationship between the Late Harappan and PGW using people. The sub-period IA at Bhagwanpura is represented by the Late Harappan culture, while the sub-period IB is marked by the continuous occupation of the Late Harappan people and the advent of the PGW using people (Joshi 1993). This overlap of two cultures is very significant and the coexistence of two different social groups tends to bridge the gap between the Late Harappan and PGW using people which is generally associated with the Aryans. In the area under present study nine sites (Ajaib-1, Bahelba-2, Ganganagar-1, Girawad-1, Kharkhra-1, Madina-2, Mokhra-3, Mokhra-5 and Seman-3) have yielded remains of both the Late Harappan and PGW periods. In absence of excavation, it is not possible to say that these sites have the same evidence as recovered from Bhagwanpura.

During the protohistoric period in the region of our current study, the last phase is characterized the PGW Culture. The exploration has yielded 22 PGW sites in the region of our study. Besides these sites, seven sites from the Rohtak Block (Kailash Kumar 1989), five from the Lakhan Majara Block (Krishan Kumar 1990) and seven from the Kalanaur Block (Lamba 1989) related to this culture have been reported. To understand the cultural history of this period, we have to depend upon two excavated sites, Daulatpur (*IAR*

1976-77: 8-9) and Bhagwanpura (Joishi 1993).

In the later Vedic period, the region of our study was a part of the Kuru kingdom. The use of iron and domestication of horse gave a key to expansion and prosperity of the kingdom and made them the paramount power of North India. In *Mahabharata* a place named 'Mahittna' is referred (*Mahabaharata* II: 3-5). 'Meham' may be corrupted from above-given name. In *Mahabharata* it is referred that Mihittna was situated in the west of Rohitiki (probably Rohtak), the capital of the Yaudheya republic. In *Mahabharata* it is referred that Nakul, the Pandava warrior (of the Kuru kingdom) conquered ten forts in the west of Khandava-Parastha. Mittittna (Meham) was one of them (*Mahabaharata* II: 29). The capital of Kurus was Indraprastha. According to H.C. Raychaudhari, Parikshita was a powerful king of the Kurus (Raychaudhari 1953: 36-37). During the age of Sixteen Mahajanapadas, the Kuru was one of the powerful janapada. The Buddhist, Jains and other literary works clearly reflect the political conditions in North India in those days (Raychaudhari 1953: 95-96 and 151).

After the age of Mahajanapadas, the region was a part of the Mauryan empire. This is attested by the discovery of an Ashoka's edict from Topra, the Yamunanagar District (Cunningham 1972-73: 140). After the decline of Mauryan empire, the region of Haryana came under the Yaudheyas. The discovery of a large number of Yaudheyas copper coins and coin moulds from Khokrakot (Sahni 1973: 76-77) proves that during the first century BCE this region was a part of the Yaudheyas republic and it was their capital and mint site.

In the end of the first century BCE, this region fell into the hands of the Indo-Greeks as evidenced by the discovery of a good number of coins and coin moulds of the Indo-Greeks from Khokhrakot (Manmohan Kumar 1996: 103), Jind (Amar Singh 1981: 296), Sonepat (*Haryana District Gazetteer* 1970: 332), Naurangabad (*IAR* 1963-64: 9), Jagadhari (Agrawala 1953: 113), Raja Karan Ka Qila, Theh Polar (Phadke 1990: 38) and Agroha (IA no.9: 130).

After the Indo-Greeks, this area comes under the rule of Sunga. Stamped pottery of Sunga period was found at Bedwa-3 and Bahelba-3. Terracotta figurines representing an elephant, which is a typical specimen of the Sunga terracotta art, were found at Bahelba-3. Towards the first century ACE the Sunga was subjugated by the Kushanas who had their kingdom in a large area of North India and the area of the present study was also included in their kingdom. In the course of exploration, a coin hoard having 68 coins was recovered from Madina-4. Besides it, Kharkara-2 has also yielded some Kushana coins (Surender Singh 1989: 49-52). Some Kushana coins have been reported from the adjoining area of our present study, such as Pakasma, Rohtak Block (Kailash Kumar 1989: 69-71), Kalanaur (Lamba 1989: 79-81), Khokhrakot (Manmohan Kumar 1996: 103) and Naurangabad (Yoganand Shastri 1999: 153).

The Kushanas were succeeded by the Yaudheyas and other tribes who had independent principalities. During the exploration, two coins of the Yaudheya of this period were found from Farmana-3. During the third and fourth centuries ACE, the Yaudheyas were ruling over a wide area, i.e. Haryana, Punjab, eastern U.P. and Bahawalpur region in Pakistan. A number of Yaudheya coins and seals has been found in the adjoining area of study area like Khokhrakot (Manmohan Kumar 1996: 100), Naurangabad (Yoganand Shastri 1999: 155), Lakhan Majra and Chandi (Krishan Kumar 1990: 51-52). The powerful Yaudheyas were defeated by Samudragupta towards the middle of the fourth century ACE. The Allahabad pillar inscription states that the Yaudheyas accepted the sovereignty of Samundragupta and their territory become a part of the great Gupta empire. Gupta coins and coin moulds have been discovered from Khokhrakot (these are housed in the Archaeological Museum of the Department of History, M.D. University, Rohtak) and Mitathal (Alteker 1957:

307).

After the Gupta empire, about in the first half of the seventh century ACE, the region was under the control of Harsa Vardhana. During the initial years of his rule, he ruled from Sthaneshwar, and afterwards he transferred his capital to Kannuaj. After the decline of Vardhanas, the Pratiharas ruled over the region of Haryana as is evident from the inscription from Pehowa (dated 882 ACE), Sirsa and Delhi of the time of Maharaja Bhojadeva (*Epigraphia Indica* XXI: 295).

After the death of Mahipal, the Tomaras and the Chahamanas became independent in northern India and established their autonomous domains. The Tomaras were the feudatories of the Pratihara rulers, as is known from the Pehowa inscription. As per the opinion of Dashartha Sharma and on the basis of the Palam-Boali and Delhi inscription, the country of Haritanka (Haryana) was ruled over by the Tomaras before the conquest by the Chahamanas and Delhi was their capital.

The Chahamana king Arnoraja (1133-51 ACE) defeated the Tomaras in the 12th century ACE. Among the Chahamana kings, Prithviraj III was the most powerful ruler. He defeated the foreign invader Muhammad Gauri in the first battle of Tarain (Trawardi) in 1191 ACE. Next year in 1192 ACE, he was defeated and killed by Gauri in the second battle of Tarain. The defeat of Prithviraj III not only changed the dynastic rule, but also forced India fall into the hands of foreigners and thus the area of our study passed under the foreign rule.

After the second battle of Tarain this region come under the rule of the Slave Dynasty. The region around Meham yielded coins of the kings of the Delhi Sultanate. This researcher found one coin of Muhammad Tughlaq from Bedwa. After sultans, the region under present study came under the rule of the Lodhi dynasty. Two coins of Sikander Saha Lodhi were found from Bedwa. Babur defeated this dynasty in the first battle at Panipat (1526) and thus laid a foundation of the great Mughal empire. The area under present study became a part of his empire. During exploration researcher found a silver coin of this dynasty from Girawad.

REFERENCE

Aggarwal, V.S. (1953) *India as known to Pānini*. Lukhnow.

Altekar, A.S. (1957) *The Coinage of the Gupta Empire*. Corpus of Indian Coins, vol.IV. Varanasi.

Amar Singh (1981) *Archaeology of Karnal and Jind District (Haryana)*. Unpublished Ph.D. Dissertation. Kurukshetra University, Kurukshetra.

Bisht, R.S. (1982) "Excavation at Banawali: 1974-77", in G.L. Possehl (ed.) *Harappan Civilization. A contemporary Perspective*. Oxford and IBH Publishing, New Delhi. pp 113-124.

Blanton, R.E. (1972) *Prehisparic Settlement Patterns of th Ixtopalopa Peninsula Region, Mexico*. Occasional Papers No. 6, Department of Anthropology, Pennsylvania State University.

Brush, J.C. and H.E. Bracy (1955) Rural Service centres in southwestern Wisconsin and southern England. *Geographical Review* 77: 599-69.

Chang, K.C. (1958) Study of the Neolithic social grouping: Examples from New World. *American Anthropologist* 60: 298-334.

Cunningham, A. (1872) *Archaeological Survey of India Reports* vol. II (1862-65). Calcutta

Cunningham, A. (1878-79) *Archaeological Survey of India Reports* vol. XIV (1862-65). Calcutta.

Duggal, S.L. (1970) *Soil Zones of Haryana*. Chaudhari-Charan Singh University Press, Hissar.

Joshi, J.P. (1993) *Excavations at Bhagwanpura 1975-76 and Other Explorations in Haryana, Jammu & Kashmir and Punjab*. Memoirs of the Archaeological Survey of India no. 89. New Delhi: Archaeological Survey of India.

Kailash Kumar (1989) *Archaeology of Lakhan Majra Block (Rohtak)*. Unpublished M.Phil Dissertation. M.D. University, Rohtak.

Khatri, J.S. and M. Acharya (1995) Kunal: A New Indus-Sarasvati Site. *Puratattva* no.25: 84-86.

Lal, B.B. (1997) *The Earliest Civilization of South Asia*. Aryan Book International, New Delhi.

Lal, B.B. (1998) *India 1947-1997: New Light on the Indus Civilization*. Aryan Book International, New Delhi.

Lal, B.B. (2000) *The Saraswati Flows on: The Continuity of Indian Culture*. Aryan Book International, New Delhi.

Lal, Makkhan (1984) *Settlement History and Rise of Civilization in Ganga-Yamuna Doab*. B.R. Publishing Corporation, New Delhi.

Lamba, Mani Ram (1989) *Archaeology and History of Kalanaur Block (Dist. Rohtak)*. Unpublished M.Phil Dissertation. M.D. University, Rohtak.

Manmohan Kumar (1996) "Ancient Mint at Rohtak" in K.K. Maheswari and Biswajeet Path (eds.), *Numismatic Panorama*. Harman Publishing House, New Delhi. pp. 95-114.

Manmohan Kumar and I.J. Naghpal (2004-05) Dispersal of Settlements of Harappan from Early Harappan to Late Harappan periods. *Puratattva* no. 34: 25-29.

Manmohan Kumar (2005-06) Recent Exploration of Harappan Sites in District Rohtak (Haryana). *Puratattva* no. 35: 196-204.

Manmohan Kumar (Mss) "Harappan Settlement in the Ghaggar-Yamuna Divide", in S.P. Gupta (ed.) *An Atlas of Indus Saraswati Civilization*.

Mughal, M.R. (1997) *Ancient Cholistan: Archaeology and Architecture*. Ferozsons, Lahore.

Nath, Amarendra (1997-98) Rakhigarhi: A Harappan Metropolis in Sarasvati-Drishadvati Divide. *Puratattva* no. 28: 39-45.

Parson, J.R. (1971) *Prehistoric Settlement Patterns in the Texcoco Region*. Memoir No. 3. University of Michigan, Museum of Anthropology, Ann Arbor.

Phadke, H.A. (1990) *Haryana: Ancient and Medieval.* Harman Publishing House, New Delhi.

Phogat, S.R. (1978) *Inscriptions of Haryana.* Kurukshetra

Rao, L.S., N.B. Sahu, Prabash Sahu, Samir Diwan and U.A. Shastry (2004-05) New light on the Excavation of Harappan Settlement at Bhirrana. *Puratattva* no. 35: 60-81.

Raychaudheri, H.C. (1953) *Political History of Ancient India.* Calcutta.

Rouse, Irving (1972) "Settlement Pattern in Archaeology", in Peter J. Ucko, Ruth Tringham and G.W. Dimbleby (eds.) *Man, Settlement and Urbanization.* London.

Sahni, Birbal (1973) *Technique of casting coins in Ancient India.* New Delhi (reprint).

Sandeep (2006) *Archaeology of Hansi Block II, District Hissar.* Unpublished M.Phil Dissertation. Kurukshetra University, Kurukshetra.

Sanders, W.T. (1956) "The Central Mexican symbiotic region: A study in prehistoric settlement pattern", in G.R. Willey (ed.) *Prehistoric Settlements Pattern in New World.* Viking Fund Publication no. 23.

Saraswati, Swami Omanand (1979) *Ancient Mints of Haryana.* Delhi (Hindi).

Sharma, A.K. (1995-96) Animal Skeletal, Remain from Mirzapur, Kurukshetra. *Puratattva* no. 26: 96-104.

Sharma, D.V., K.C. Nauryal, V.N. Prabhakar and Vishnu Kant (2004-05) Sanauli: A Late Harappan Burial Site in the Yamuna-Hindon Doab. *Puratattva* no.34: 35-44.

Sheela Devi (1978) *Art Traditions in Haryana.* Unpublished Ph.D. Thesis. Kurukshetra University, Kurukshetra.

Silak Ram (1972) *Archaeology of Rohtak and Hissar District (Haryana).* Unpublished Ph.D. thesis. Kurukshetra University, Kurukshetra.

Singh, U.V. (1976) "Recent Archaeological Discoveries in the Vicinity of Thanesar", *Kurukshetra University Research Journal* X.

Suraj, Bhan (1975) *Excavation at Mitathal (1968) and other Exploration in Sutlej-Yamuna Divide.* Kurukshetra University, Kurukshetra.

Surender Singh (1989) *History and Archaeology of Meham Block, District Rohtak.* Unpublished M.Phil Dissertation. M.D. University, Rohtak.

Thomas, E.N. (1961) The Stability of Distance Population Size Relationship for Ivoa Towns from 1900 to 1950. *Land Studies in Geography Series, B. Human Geography* no. 24: 13-30.

Trigger, B.G. (1965) *Historic and Settlement in lower Nubia.* Yale University Publication in Anthropology no. 67 (2).

Trigger, B.G. (1967) Settlement Archaeology its goal and Promise. *American Antiquity* no. 32: 151.

Tringham, Ruth (1972)" Settlement Pattern in Archaeology", in Peter J. Ucko, Ruth Tringham and G.W. Dimbleby (eds.) *Man, Settlement and Urbanization.* London.

Willey, G.R. (1953) *Prehistoric Settlements Patterns in Virus Valley, Peru.* Bulletin of Bureau of American Ethnology. Washington D.C.

Yoganand Shastri (1999) *Prachin Bharat Me Yaudheya Ganrajya.* Bhagwat Lazer Prints, New Delhi.